Innovationsmanagement und Entrepreneurship

Herausgegeben von
R. Gleich,
P. Spieth,
F. Täube,
Oestrich-Winkel, Deutschland

In unserer Schriftenreihe „Innovationsmanagement und Entrepreneurship" werden wichtige Ergebnisse der wissenschaftlichen und praxisorientierten Forschung des Strascheg Institute for Innovation and Entrepreneurship (SIIE) der EBS Business School veröffentlicht.

Our series includes excellent academic and practitioner oriented research in the area of innovation management and entrepreneurship which has been recently conducted at EBS Business School, Strascheg Institute for Innovation and Entrepreneurship (SIIE).

Herausgegeben von
Prof. Dr. Ronald Gleich,
Prof. Dr. Patrick Spieth,
Prof. Dr. Florian Täube,
EBS Business School, EBS Universität für Wirtschaft und Recht,
Strascheg Institut für Innovation und Entrepreneurship (SIIE),
Oestrich-Winkel, Deutschland

Michael Migendt

Accelerating Green Innovation

Essays on Alternative Investments in Clean Technologies

Foreword by Prof. Dr. Ronald Gleich

Springer Gabler

Michael Migendt
Oestrich-Winkel, Germany

Dissertation EBS Universität für Wirtschaft und Recht – EBS Business School, Oestrich-Winkel, 2015

Innovationsmanagement und Entrepreneurship
ISBN 978-3-658-17250-3 ISBN 978-3-658-17251-0 (eBook)
DOI 10.1007/978-3-658-17251-0

Library of Congress Control Number: 2017931354

Springer Gabler

Printed on acid-free paper

This Springer Gabler imprint is published by Springer Nature
The registered company is Springer Fachmedien Wiesbaden GmbH
The registered company address is: Abraham-Lincoln-Str. 46, 65189 Wiesbaden, Germany

Foreword

The work of Dr. Michael Migendt focuses on the role of regulation and the influence of private investors in the development of clean technology markets in the USA and Europe. Core to those are for example wind and solar energy technologies that enable a sustainable use of the earth's resources. A special topic of this work is the changing role of finance and policy along the cleantech innovation chain.

These two main topics in Mr. Migendt's work were embedded in a research initiative of the German federal government (supported by the federal Ministry of Education and Research) with the title "Climate Change, Financial Markets and Innovation" (CFI). This initiative focused on diverse questions in the field of clean technology markets like innovation, regulation & policy making as well as finance.

Alternative investments were core of the research activities at the Strascheg Institut for Innovation and Entrepreneurship (SIIE) within the BMBF research project. These are commonly known and applied as private equity and venture capital finance.

The present work was one of three dissertation projects at my institute at the EBS Universität für Wirtschaft und Recht in the foresaid context and has its special focus on "green policy for green innovation" with another focus on the commercialization phase of innovations. The other dissertations in contrast focus on the earlier innovation phase (generation - Dissertation Dr. Friedemann Polzin) respectively later innovation phase (diffusion – Dr. Florian Schock).

The work of Dr. Michael Migendt is valuable source of advice for researchers, policy makers and investors regarding to innovation, investments and clean technology activities.

Prof. Dr. Ronald Gleich

Acknowledgements

4 years – 3 universities – 5 co-authors – 8 countries – 100s of interviews – 100,000s of articles – 1 dissertation

This dissertation represents the outcome of my research work conducted at the Strascheg Institute for Innovation and Entrepreneurship (SIIE) at EBS Universität für Wirtschaft und Recht in Wiesbaden. I am very thankful to all those that have supported me throughout this time and happy to conclude my thesis not only with a degree, but with many valuable new friendships and memorable experiences.

First of all, I am indebted to Prof. Ronald Gleich for his support, advice, and the academic freedom he provided during my time at SIIE. I would also like to thank Prof. Florian Täube for being my key research advisor and co-author of my papers. His ideas, guidance and priceless connections to the academic world made this thesis and accompanying projects possible.

My thesis would also not have been possible without the support of the Climate Change, Financial Markets and Innovation (CFI) research project funded by the German Ministry for Research and Education (BMBF). As head of the CFI research project, a special thank you to the Director of the Sustainable Business Institute (SBI) and co-author of my research papers, Dr. Paschen von Flotow, whose advice, industry insights and experiences proved to be invaluable for the success of this dissertation.

My special appreciation and thanks go to my co-authors Dr. Friedemann Polzin and Dr. Florian Schock. Through strong collaboration, innumerable hours of interviewing, analyzing and data crunching, as well as, lots of inspiring discussions we managed to complete a challenging research project and our dissertations.

A big thank you to Prof. Brett Gilbert from Rutgers University, who is not only my co-author but also an inspiring role model for my academic work. Her valuable input, innovative approaches and comprehensive knowledge pushed our common work forward.

I am very grateful to Prof. Zhang Wei and Prof. Steven White from Tsinghua University - School of Economics and Management, who hosted me during my research stay in Beijing and not only offered me generous support and valuable insights, but also integrated me in the research culture at Tsinghua University.

My sincere thanks to Prof. Martin Kenney and Don Patton from the University of California, Davis - Department of Human Ecology who hosted me during my research stay in California and offered academic insights, help with the last mile of my dissertation and made me feel remarkably welcome.

A special thank you to all my colleagues at SIIE and SBI. Their support, companionship, time for a talk and a laugh have been indispensable.

Thank you to the discussion partners all over the world who took their time to support our research and provide us with unparalleled insights in the world of finance, innovation and clean technologies.

Key to this dissertation were also my friends who supported me throughout this time. Many thanks to them.

Finally, I cannot express in words how grateful I am towards my family who have made this dissertation possible and supported me throughout the years.

Thank you.

Michael Migendt

Table of Contents

Foreword V

Acknowledgements VII

Table of Contents IX

List of Figures XIII

List of Tables XV

List of Abbreviations XVII

1 Introduction 1

1.1 Motivation, purpose and scope 1

1.2 Research context 2

1.3 Research questions and methodology 5

2 Emergence of Cleantech as an Investment Category - Media Attention and Venture Capital Investment 9

2.1 Introduction 9

2.2 Theory 11

2.2.1 Venture Capital Evolution 11

2.2.2 Venture Capital Life Cycle 12

2.2.3 Cleantech Venture Capital 13

2.3 Research methodology & data 15

2.3.1 Data 15

2.3.2 Method 16

2.4 Results and discussion 18

2.4.1 The cleantech venture capital life cycle 18

2.4.2 Early Investment Stage 21

2.4.3 Commitment Stage 22

2.4.4 Institutionalization Stage 23

2.4.5 Overshooting Stage 25

2.4.6 Stabilization Stage 26
2.5 Conclusion 28
2.6 Acknowledgements 29
3 Private Equity in Clean Technology: An Exploratory Study of the Finance-Innovation-Policy Nexus 31
3.1 Introduction 31
3.2 Theoretical Background 33
3.2.1 Role of the finance eco-system for innovation 33
3.2.2 Public policy influence on the finance-innovation relationship 35
3.3 Method and Data 37
3.3.1 Research Context 38
3.3.2 Data Collection 40
3.3.3 Data analysis 42
3.4 Findings 44
3.4.1 Innovation policy (direct and indirect) effects 44
3.4.2 Financial policy (direct and indirect) effects 49
3.5 Discussion 53
3.5.1 Financing innovation beyond VC/PE – the role of institutional investors 53
3.5.2 Unintended policy consequences in financing industry emergence – the case of US and German cleantech markets 54
3.6 Conclusions and policy implications 56
3.7 Acknowledgements 58
4 Public policy influence on renewable energy investments – a panel data study across OECD countries 59
4.1 Introduction 59
4.2 Theoretical background 61
4.2.1 Public policy influence on renewable energy deployment 61
4.2.2 Investors' perspective on renewable energies 64

4.3 Methods and data ... 66
4.3.1 Research design ... 66
4.3.2 Data ... 66
4.3.3 Model ... 68
4.3.4 Longitudinal analysis (panel data regression) ... 70
4.4 Results and discussion ... 72
4.4.1 Fiscal and financial incentives ... 75
4.4.2 Market-based incentives ... 76
4.4.3 Direct investments ... 78
4.4.4 Policy support ... 79
4.4.5 Regulatory instruments ... 80
4.4.6 Robustness checks ... 80
4.5 Conclusions and policy implications ... 81
4.6 Acknowledgements ... 82
5 Development of Industries in the Cleantech Sector - A Case of the Solar and Fuel Cell Industries ... 83
5.1 Introduction ... 83
5.2 Theoretical framework ... 84
5.3 Research methodology & data ... 86
5.3.1 Cases of industry evolution ... 86
5.3.2 Data ... 87
5.3.3 Method ... 88
5.4 Results and discussion ... 89
5.5 Concluding remarks ... 93
6 Conclusion ... 95
6.1 Accelerating green innovation through alternative investments ... 95
6.2 The changing role of finance and policy along the cleantech innovation chain ... 96
6.3 Implications for investors and innovators ... 97

6.4 Policy implications ... 98
6.5 Limitations and suggestions for future research ... 99
7 References ... 103
8 Appendix ... 129
8.1 Appendix to chapter 2 ... 129
8.2 Appendix to chapter 3 ... 130
8.3 Appendix to chapter 4 ... 140
8.4 Appendix to chapter 5 ... 146

List of Figures

Figure 1 – Role of innovation, finance, and policy in the innovation chain 4
Figure 2 – Historical development of articles containing the term "Venture Capital" 15
Figure 3 – Venture capital investments - total and cleantech from 1995 to 2013.... 18
Figure 4 – Total venture capital articles and deals from 1995 to 2011 19
Figure 5 – Cleantech venture capital articles and deals from 1995 to 2011 20
Figure 6 – Dictionary application – sector importance in venture capital articles... 21
Figure 7 – Global VC/PE investment in CT by stage in USD bn 32
Figure 8 – Theoretical framework 37
Figure 9 – Global new investment in CT in USD bn 38
Figure 10 – New investment in CT (USA and GER) in USD bn 40
Figure 11 – Coding Process 42
Figure 12 – Example of coding process 43
Figure 13 – Final model including relationships (based on findings) 54
Figure 14 – Renewable power capacity investment compared to fossil-fuel power capacity investment, 2008-2013 in billion USD. 60
Figure 15 – Model for the quantitative panel regression 68
Figure 16 – Industry deals and article 89
Figure 17 – Sector frames „solar energy“ 90
Figure 18 – Sector frames "fuel cell" 91
Figure 19 – Investment stage funding "solar energy" (in mUSD) 92
Figure 20 – Investment stage funding "fuel cell" (in mUSD) 92
Figure 21 – Cleantech dictionary 129
Figure 22 – Dictionaries used on articles 146
Figure 23 – Technology frames "solar energy" 146
Figure 24 – Technology frames "fuel cell" 146

List of Tables

Table 1 – Overview chapters of dissertation ... 7
Table 2 – Correlation of VC general and CT – articles vs. investments ... 19
Table 3 – Description of life cycle phases ... 27
Table 4 – Key actors in the finance-innovation eco-system (definitions) ... 34
Table 5 – Overview of policy measures discussed ... 36
Table 6 – Overview of Interviews in the United States and Germany ... 41
Table 7 – Perceptions of innovation policy for CT ... 49
Table 8 – Perceptions of financial policy affecting CT ... 52
Table 9 – Specification tests for the quantitative model ... 71
Table 10 – Panel-corrected Standard Errors (PCSE) Regression Results ... 73
Table 11 – Ordinary Least Square (OLS) Regression Results ... 74
Table 12 – Overview about the results ... 78
Table 13 – Correlation table article & investments ... 90
Table 14 – Innovation policy (direct and indirect) effects ... 133
Table 15 – Financial policy (direct and indirect) effects ... 136
Table 16 – Detailed interview descriptives ... 138
Table 17 – Country selection ... 140
Table 18 – Data: definition, sources and descriptive statistics ... 142
Table 19 – Pairwise correlation coefficients (Multiple RE /aggregated sectors) ... 143
Table 20 – Random effects estimator (REE) regression results ... 144

List of Abbreviations

ANPM	-	Accumulated number of RE policies and measures
ARPA-E	-	Advanced Research Projects Agency - Energy
BNEF	-	Bloomberg New Energy Finance
BRIC	-	Brazil, Russia, India and China
CalPERS	-	California Public Employees' Retirement System
CalSTRS	-	California State Teachers' Retirement System
CEO	-	Chief executive officer
CT	-	Cleantech
DOE	-	Department of energy
ERISA	-	Employee retirement income security act
EU	-	European Union
FIT	-	Feed-in tariffs
GDP	-	Gross domestic product
GHG	-	Greenhouse gas
GP	-	General partner
IEA	-	International Energy Agency
IPCC	-	Intergovernmental Panel on Climate Change
IPO	-	Initial public offering
IRENA	-	International Renewable Energy Agency
LDC	-	Less developed countries
LGP	-	Loan guarantee program
M&A	-	Mergers & Acquisitions
MLP	-	Multi-level perspective
NIS	-	National innovation system
NREL	-	National renewable energy laboratory
OECD	-	Organisation for Economic Co-operation and Development
OLS	-	Ordinary least squares
PCSE	-	Panel corrected standard error

PE	-	Private equity
PM	-	Policy and Measures
PPP	-	Public private partnership
R&D	-	Research and development
RD&D	-	Research, development and demonstration
RE	-	Renewable energy
REE	-	Random effects estimator
ROC	-	Renewable obligation certificates
RPS	-	Renewable portfolio standards
SBIR	-	Small Business Innovation Research
SME	-	Small and medium sized enterprise
SOFC	-	Solid oxide fuel cell
TIS	-	Technological innovation system
VC	-	Venture capital

1 Introduction

1.1 Motivation, purpose and scope

Innovation in clean technologies is key to green growth. The possibilities to support a sustainable economic environment have been under scrutiny by policymakers and researchers in recent years (Heck, Rogers, & Carroll, 2014; Mowery, Nelson, & Martin, 2010a; OECD, 2011; Stern, 2006). Important factors to achieve a transition to a more sustainable economy include policy and financial support. Governments and international organizations have been actively supporting environmentalism and clean technologies for decades. Since the 1990s a trend towards sustainability, especially in the ecological sense has emerged. Based on this fact, the financial sector and likewise entrepreneurial ventures, have recognized the economic value of this trend. New products, services, and processes with an environmentally friendly mindset are being developed (Foxon & Pearson, 2008b; Markard, Raven, & Truffer, 2012; Pernick & Wilder, 2007). Calls for further support from governments and private actors seek to accelerate green innovation.[1] Finance, especially private finance as a means to bridge gaps and circumvent barriers is seen as one possible solution (Altenburg & Pegels, 2012; Mazzucato & Perez, 2014; OECD, 2011).

Finance for young innovative companies in the clean technology space is most often invested through alternative asset classes. Alternative investments (alternative to traditional public equity and bond investments) are expected to provide better returns and/or diversification of risk. Main categories within alternative investments are typically real estate, infrastructure, hedge funds, commodities, private equity (PE) and venture capital (VC). This thesis focuses on investments in private equity, venture capital and energy, which is a part of infrastructure, to analyze finance for green innovations (Fraser-Sampson, 2011; Greer, 1997; Kaminker & Stewart, 2012).

---

1 Green innovation is defined by technologies that focus on sustainability, mitigation and adaptation to climate change, or reduction of natural resources. For example, these clean technologies and renewable energy solutions are: solar or wind energy technologies, electric cars, energy efficiency technology and other smart resource reduction approaches. Not only products, but also business models and process or service innovations can be green innovations (Caprotti, 2012; O'Rourke, 2009; Pernick & Wilder, 2007).

It uses a broad spectrum of qualitative and quantitative data on the alternative investment and clean technology sectors to find an answer to how to accelerate green innovation. Building on extensive interviews, conference visits, as well as, data from various financial databases, newspaper archives and policy reports, the following chapters show a comprehensive picture of the clean technology innovation system. The changing role of finance and policy along the clean technology innovation chain is scrutinized to understand the evolution of the associated industries. In addition to the contribution to academic literature, the thesis also derives implications for investors, innovators, and policy makers. The dissertation, consequently, contributes to the research debate on how to accelerate green innovation and as well on the role of finance and policy in the clean technology innovation chain (Altenburg & Pegels, 2012; Mazzucato & Perez, 2014; Wüstenhagen & Menichetti, 2012).

1.2 Research context

The overarching aim of this thesis is to explain the role of alternative investments in supporting the growth of a sustainable economy and recognizing levers that policymakers, managers and entrepreneurs could use for further accelerating green innovation through finance. Thus, it considers the activity of VC, PE and infrastructure investments in the field of clean technologies and renewable energies, and furthermore, looks for possible policy measures and regulatory interventions to strengthen the investment environment. Accelerating green innovation for a more sustainable future and a transition to a green economy has been a consistent request recently (Heck et al., 2014; Mowery et al., 2010a; OECD, 2011; Stern, 2006).

The clean technology industry emerged over the recent decades. Patterns of technological change and the entry of new innovative firms into the industry constitute this development. Lack of legitimacy is a key problem in the early years of an industry and has to develop though the help of emerging institutions. Based on the maturing clean technology industry a sustainability transition of the economy has been enabled (Aldrich & Fiol, 1994; Audretsch, 1995; Avnimelech & Teubal, 2006; Hoffman, 1999; F. Malerba, Nelson, Orsenigo, & Winter, 1999). The transition to green industries is a socio-technical transition changing not only technologies but also institutional structures and user practices. This change is triggered by innovation on the one hand and by policy changes induced by cultural shifts on the other hand. "Sustainability transitions are long-term, multi-dimensional, and fundamental transformation processes through which established socio-technical systems shift to more sustainable modes of production and consumption" (Markard et al., 2012, p. 956). The sustainability transition is key to accelerating green innovations (Farla, Markard,

Raven, & Coenen, 2012; Hoppmann, Huenteler, & Girod, 2014; Jacobsson & Bergek, 2004; Markard et al., 2012; A. Smith, Voß, & Grin, 2010).

External sources of finance, VC or PE, as well as, public financing activities have played a crucial role in the development of many innovative technologies and emerging industries (Kenney, 2011a; Mazzucato, 2013a; O'Sullivan, 2005; Perez, 2002a; Wonglimpiyarat, 2011; Samara, Georgiadis, & Bakouros, 2012; Mina, Lahr, & Hughes, 2013; Hirsch-Kreinsen, 2011). Challenges associated with the transition towards a low-carbon economy are multifaceted. But lack of financing has proven to be one of the major barriers for green innovation (Howell, 2014; Iyer et al., 2015; Leete, Xu, & Wheeler, 2013; Stucki, 2014). Regulatory interventions have been administered to amend such barriers like market failures and stimulate environmental innovation in clean industries (U. C. Haley & Schuler, 2011; Veugelers, 2012a).

Green innovation in the manifestation of clean technologies will play a key role for this transition (for a literature review on green innovation, see Schiederig, Tietze, & Herstatt, 2012). This thesis focuses on industries usually classified in the clean technology or renewable energy sector. Nevertheless, the boundaries of the so called clean technology sector are not definitive. Researchers found ways to describe the variety of included market participants. A comprehensive yet illustrative definition by O'Rourke explains: "Cleantech companies develop, produce and disseminate goods and services that improve the environmental performance of the system to which they are applied." (2009, p. 109) (Caprotti, 2012; O'Rourke, 2009; Pernick & Wilder, 2007).

This thesis looks at the interplay of finance, innovation, and policy along the innovation chain (see Figure 1) and focuses on possible means to accelerate green innovation. The stages technology generation, technology commercialization and technology diffusion and their corresponding financial or policy measures are the backbone to this work. The changing innovation environment demands for specific financial sources and targeted policy measures (Auerswald & Branscomb, 2003; Borrás & Edquist, 2013; Brown, 1990; Wüstenhagen & Menichetti, 2012).

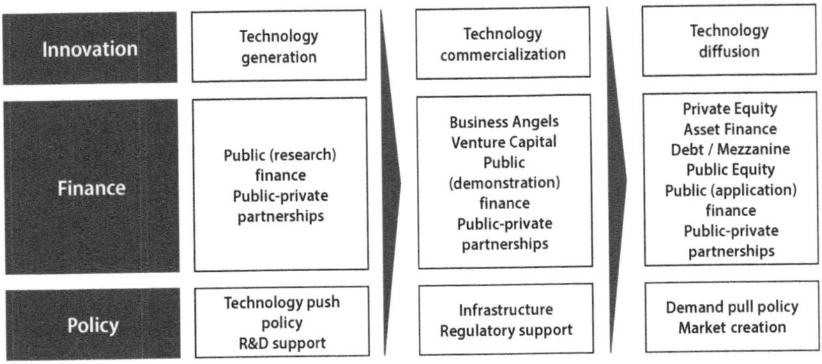

Figure 1 – Role of innovation, finance, and policy in the innovation chain

During the technology generation stage main sources for finance are mostly of public origin or combinations of public and private origin. Especially in the transition from science to business, the public actors need to be heavily involved (Pisano, 2010). R&D is a costly endeavor, and more often support mechanisms from regulators have to support innovation efforts. In the generation phase, technology push policies have to strengthen the innovation environment (Peters, Schneider, Griesshaber, & Hoffmann, 2012a; Samara et al., 2012). Nevertheless, picking winners or losers through government policy should be avoided (Aghion, David, & Foray, 2009; Åhman, 2006).

Public policy and financing support can still play a role in risky areas of the technology commercialization stage. Still, private investments through business angels, venture capitalists and public-private partnership investments take over during that stage (Brown, 1990; Oakey, 2003). The private risk investors play an important role. While they take risk they expect adjusted returns in exchange. Limiting the availability of private finance is the so-called "Valley of Death". Market acceptance risks and scaling risks diminish return expectancies and discourage angel and VC investors (Auerswald & Branscomb, 2003; Da Rin, Hellmann, & Puri, 2011; Miller & Garnsey, 2000). Especially through this situation the importance of private risk capital investors for supporting innovation and entrepreneurship in the commercialization stage is emphasized. Hence, regulatory interventions appear to be able to bridge this financing gap (Samila & Sorenson, 2010a).

In the clean technology field, diffusion is hindered by a multitude of different barriers (Negro, Alkemade, & Hekkert, 2012; Tsoutsos & Stamboulis, 2005). Even as most technology risks and market acceptance risks have been resolved, finance is still a problematic issue. Thus, clean technology and renewable energy technologies are heavily subsidized even at later stages of the innovation chain (Badcock & Lenzen, 2010; Bolinger, Wiser, Milford, Stoddard, & Porter, 2001) These policy interventions have shown to have high influence on inducing green innovations, especially conducive are demand pull mechanisms (Barreto & Kemp, 2007; Peters et al., 2012a; Veugelers, 2012a) In contrast, high regulatory exposure can prevent investors from financing clean technologies (Chassot, Hampl, & Wüstenhagen, 2014). Maturing financial markets play a role especially in later stages of technology diffusion. Less risky types of financing take over during the diffusion stage, while private equity, infrastructure and partly public equity gain importance (Comin & Nanda, 2014).

1.3 Research questions and methodology

In order to provide an insightful analysis, the following chapters emphasize important aspects of alternative investments in clean technologies. Each chapter focuses on specific examples of alternative investments into green industries, companies, projects, and infrastructure, covering the developments along the innovation chain. Especially the acceleration of green technologies and the in this context occurring interrelations between the three areas of finance, innovation, and policy are key to this work:

Chapter 2 introduces the topic of investments into clean technologies from a VC viewpoint. It tells the historic emergence of the investment category and develops a life-cycle model for the industry. It thus is a key component to understand the transition towards sustainability (Markard et al., 2012; Penna & Geels, 2012). To analyze the historical events in the development, the chapter uses a longitudinal approach (Da Rin et al., 2011; Elo & Kyngäs, 2007; Navis & Glynn, 2010; Wright, Pruthi, & Lockett, 2005). A quantitative and qualitative content analysis of newspaper articles combined with investment data shows technology emergence patterns and detailed information on trending topics (Hoffman, 1999; Kennedy, 2005; McGrath, 1998). The chapter adds a systemic overview over the historic development of the industry evolution to the research debate. It recognized, that the investment category developed according to a venture capital life-cycle model with distinct stages (Avnimelech, Kenney, & Teubal, 2004; Avnimelech & Teubal, 2006). Through the analysis, the historical development and as well the suitability of cleantech VC as an investments category is regarded (Randjelovic, O'Rourke, & Orsato, 2003; Ghosh & Nanda, 2010; Kenney, 2011b; Marcus, Malen, & Ellis, 2013).

The research question chapter 2 answers is as follows:

How does an investment category within venture capital emerge?

Chapter 3 investigates direct and indirect effects of financial policy and innovation-oriented policies in the cleantech area in a cross-country comparison (Borrás & Edquist, 2013; Brossard, Lavigne, & Sakinç, 2013a; Flanagan, Uyarra, & Laranja, 2011a; Grilli & Murtinu, 2014; Kenney, 2011b; Revest & Sapio, 2013; Veugelers, 2012b; Wonglimpiyarat, 2011). It uses an exploratory, qualitative study based on interviews in the US and Europe. Interviewees were VC and PE investors, as well as, institutional investors, policy makers and entrepreneurs from the industry (Bewley, 2002; K. Eisenhardt, 1989; Jick, 1979). The chapter contributes to the research debate by incorporating the mobilization of finance for (cleantech) innovation. Adding institutional investors as important actors shaping the conditions for innovation by investing into VC/PE firms it identifies unintended consequences at the intersection between financial sector and innovating firms (Mathews, Kidney, Mallon, & Hughes, 2010a; Mazzucato, 2013a; Mina et al., 2013; Stucki, 2014).

Chapter 3 answers the following research question:

How does the interplay between equity finance and corresponding policy measures influence (cleantech) innovation and entrepreneurship?

Chapter 4 examines the impact of public policy measures on renewable energy (RE) investments in electricity-generating capacity. It thus adds to the debate of how to support the renewable energy transition (Hoppmann et al., 2014; Jacobsson & Bergek, 2004; Markard et al., 2012). Using a novel combination of datasets and conducting a panel data regression, it analyzes effective policy measures to encourage RE investments by institutional investors (Cárdenas-Rodríguez, Johnstone, Haščič, Silva, & Ferey, 2013; Marques & Fuinhas, 2012a, 2012b).

The results of this chapter call for technology-specific policies which take into account actual market conditions and position in the technology life cycle.

Chapter 4 answers the following research question:

Which policies have proven (most) conducive to investments in renewable energy assets?

Chapter 5 compares the role of innovation, finance and policy for the development of cleantech industries. Therefore it contributes to the perspective of sustainability transitions and to the industry development changes along the innovation chain (Borrás & Edquist, 2013; Brown, 1990; Jacobsson & Bergek, 2011; Wüstenhagen & Menichetti, 2012). Explaining the historical development of the solar energy and fuel cell industries, it depicts the peculiarities of green growth. A quantitative content analysis of press articles from US newspapers is used to analyze the different topics during the period from 1995 to 2013 (Aghion et al., 2009; Autio, Kenney, Mustar, Siegel, & Wright, 2014; Geels, 2014; Mazzucato, 2013a; Miller & Garnsey, 2000).

The chapter observes the changing relevance of the specific actors during industry development and compares results of the solar energy to the fuel cell industry. This chapter helps explain the importance of a technology specific and life-cycle adjusted regulatory environment to overcome barriers in the transition to a green economy (Altenburg & Pegels, 2012; Foxon & Pearson, 2008b).

The main research question of chapter 5 is:

What role do innovation, investments and policy play in the development of (cleantech) industries?

Table 1 provides an overview of the articles joined together as chapters of this thesis and provides insights on the corresponding research questions methodological approaches and data sources used:

	Title	Research question	Method	Data
2	Emergence of Cleantech as an Investment Category - Media Attention and Venture Capital Investment	How does an investment category within venture capital emerge?	Qualitative/Quantitative – Longitudinal media/investment analysis	84,259 global newspaper articles from LexisNexis Investment data on deals and investment sum from Thomson One Period: 1995 - 2013
3	Private Equity in Clean Technology: An Exploratory Study of the Finance-Innovation-Policy Nexus	How does the interplay between equity finance and corresponding policy measures influence (cleantech) innovation and entrepreneurship?	Qualitative – interview based	64 interviews with VC/PE investors, limited partners, policy makers & entrepreneurs in the USA and Europe Period: 2011 - 2012
4	Public policy influence on renewable energy investments – a panel data study across OECD countries	Which policies have proven (most) conducive to investments in renewable energy assets?	Quantitative – Cross-sectional panel study	18,372 renewable energy investments from Bloomberg New Energy Finance 957 policies from IEA/IRENA Policy and Measures (PM) database Period: 2000-2011
5	Development of Cleantech Industries – A Media Analysis of the Solar Energy and Fuel Cell Industries	What role do innovation, investments and policy play in the development of (cleantech) industries?	Quantitative – Longitudinal media/investment analysis	5,356 US newspaper articles from LexisNexis Investment data on deals and investment sum from Thomson One Period: 1995 - 2013

Table 1 – Overview chapters of dissertation

The uniqueness of this thesis, is based on the multitude of approaches and data foundations used to contribute to the research debate. A mix of qualitative and quantitative research designs is used in the different chapters. Longitudinal and cross-sectional studies help to explain complex evolutionary or multi-actor settings. In addition, deploying a vast variety of different data sources prevents from possible biases and enriches the depth of the analysis. Several databases containing financial, policy, and newspaper information have been consulted. Moreover interviews with market participants have been led.

2 Emergence of Cleantech as an Investment Category – Media Attention and Venture Capital Investment

Authors: Michael Migendt, Florian A. Täube, Brett A. Gilbert & Paschen von Flotow

Abstract:

This paper investigates the emergence of the category "clean technology investing" in the field of venture capital (VC). Building on industry evolution and life-cycle literature it extends the understanding of drivers for VC growth. It takes industry and public policy forces into account. The case of cleantech investing is examined using a multitude of datasets and methods including a quantitative and qualitative content analysis. A software-based analysis of press publications combined with investment data shows clean technology media and investment emergence patterns. These patterns follow evolutionary life-cycle patterns. The paper conjectures on factors that influence observed patterns in each stage.

2.1 Introduction

Sustainability and cleantech are commonplace words today relative to two decades ago. Renewable energy, energy efficiency and alternative transportation technologies which are part of the cleantech vernacular originate from inventions from the 1980s and 1990s and were developed to become household knowledge and important business sectors (Pernick & Wilder, 2007). The term cleantech was created by the investment community and is widely regarded as a major investment category or even asset class (Caprotti, 2012; O'Rourke, 2009; Pernick & Wilder, 2007). The cleantech industry encompasses companies that focus on green and sustainable technologies with product, process or service offerings decreasing the amount of greenhouse gas emissions. Newly introduced technologies such as cleantech require significant work to establish their positioning within society. This development is carried heavily by small, innovative, and entrepreneurial ventures (Hockerts & Wüstenhagen, 2010a), which commonly lack the resources that are needed for rapid growth. Venture capitalists have developed a strong reputation for funding promising technology companies. For this reason, entrepreneurial firms are commonly financed by venture capitalists (VCs) who provide the requisite capital. VCs provide funding that is not generally available through traditional financial institutions, and have been found to be one of the major drivers of innovation and technology commercialization (Da Rin et al., 2011; Samila & Sorenson, 2010a).They are especially important during early stages of an industry. For example, von Burg and Kenney (2000) describes the emergence of the local area network (LAN) industry and the support provided through VC. According to their work, not only did the VCs supply capital for the companies but also assisted in strategic planning and were influential over the adoption of a dominant design. Dodgson et al. (2008) similarly highlighted the role and importance of VC in the evolution of the national as well as sectoral innovation system (NIS/SIS) in Taiwan's biotech industry. Despite these studies, there is limited research that shows how new technology classes are financed over time by the VC community.

This article explores the evolution of the cleantech category for venture capital investment from early industry emergence to a decline in investment. While cleantech as a new industry and its corresponding investment category has been reviewed in recent research, a comprehensive analysis of the category's investment evolution has not been done (Randjelovic et al., 2003; Ghosh & Nanda, 2010; Kenney, 2011b; Marcus et al., 2013; Cumming, Henriques, & Sadorsky, 2013). This paper seeks to explain when an investment category within venture capital emerges and the factors associated with its evolution. It leverages longitudinal data including press articles mentioning "venture capital" from Lexis Nexis to analyze the emergence of the cleantech VC category (Da Rin, Hellmann, and Puri 2011; Wright, Pruthi, and Lockett 2005). These articles are analyzed alongside investment data from Thomson One Banker to identify key milestones of investment class emergence and to understand how investment patterns align with or deviate with media attention given to emerging technology classes. Cleantech terminology within media data is used to identify investment stages and the technologies, that dominated the stages of industry development (Hoffman, 1999; Kennedy, 2005; Navis & Glynn, 2010).

By analyzing the historical emergence of the cleantech VC category, this paper shows patterns relevant for emerging investments within the VC industry. Moreover, there is a gap in academic literature showing historical patterns of VC investments (Da Rin, Hellmann, and Puri 2011; Wright, Pruthi, and Lockett 2005). This study adds to the different streams of literature and addresses calls for further research by (1) Gompers and Lerner (2001) who asked for additional research on the interlink between the growth of the VC industry and the respective funded high-tech companies; (2) Wüstenhagen and Teppo (Wüstenhagen & Teppo, 2006) who requested more work on the emergence of market sectors within VC especially with a focus on cleantech; and (3) Avnimelech et al. (2004) who see opportunities to transfer their life cycle model to different areas of application.

The main research question of this paper is:

How does an investment category within venture capital emerge?

The paper proceeds as follows. It begins with a theoretical background on venture capital evolution and life cycle. It then describes the data and research methods used, followed by results of the analysis from the media database matched with the investment data. It concludes with a discussion on the emergence and evolution of the cleantech venture capital category, the paper's limitations and several suggestions for future research.

2.2 Theory

2.2.1 Venture Capital Evolution

VCs play essential roles in funding the commercialization of new technologies. Thus, the emergence of a VC investment category is important for technological innovation and business formation (Florida & Kenney, 1988a, 1988b; Lerner, 2002; Oakey, 2003; Samila & Sorenson, 2010a; Timmons & Bygrave, 1986). Despite this importance, there has been "little research ...[on] the industrial organization of the VC industry and its evolution over time." (Da Rin et al., 2011, p. 100). The creation of markets is typically described as an evolutionary development in a systemic environment (Hekkert et al., 2007; Nelson & Winter, 1982). Karaomerlioglu and Jacobsson (2000, p. 77) argue that "a VC industry evolves as a function of the institutional set-up in the economy".

In national contexts, government policy influences evolutionary development of VC investment classes and the overall VC industry (Lerner, 2009; S. White, Gao, & Zhang, 2005). White et al. (2005) confirms the importance of governments creating a macroeconomic environment that supports a national venture capital industry. A VC industry also requires a sufficiently active entrepreneurial community for investments as well as open capital markets for exiting investments (Da Rin, Nicodano, & Sembenelli, 2006a; Jeng & Wells, 2000; Kenney, 2011a).

In contrast to the institutionalized VC markets in the USA, Israel and Taiwan, research on VC market growth in the German, European, Hong Kong, and Swedish VC markets (Becker & Hellmann, 2003; Bottazzi & Da Rin, 2002; Chu & Hisrich, 2001; Karaomerlioglu & Jacobsson, 2000) and Asian markets (Dossani & Kenney, 2002; Kenney, Han, & Tanaka,, 2004) shows that internal and external forces drive the VC market evolution. Industry level research has examined several aspects of general VC historic development or its development in certain countries and regions. It reveals cyclicality in the investment process, the level of funding, as well as the returns on subsequent investments (Bygrave, Fast, Khoylian, Vincent, & William, 1989; Gompers & Lerner, 2001). For example, Murray (1995) concludes that by the mid of the 1990s the VC industry as a whole had reached a maturity stage as described in Porter's (1980) model of industry maturity. To ensure a future path for the industry, investments into new industries or categories is necessary (Badino, Hu, & Hung, 2006). For this reason, VC investments follow a life-cycle process, where investments begin, grow and decline over time.

2.2.2 Venture Capital Life Cycle

Kenney (2011a) compares the development of VC to the emergence of an organizational ecology. Thus, the growth of VC as an institution can be compared to an evolutionary process and the analysis of its creation requires a systemic perspective. Building on emergence and industry formation literature (e.g. Abernathy & Utterback, 1978; Klepper, 1996, 1997; Franco Malerba & Orsenigo, 1996) Avnimelech, Kenney, and Teubal (2004) suggest that high-tech industries in the USA and Israel co-evolve with adjoining VC-markets. The authors build a life cycle model reflecting the emergence and evolution of these VC industries and describe it "as a cumulative, self-reinforcing process with a distinctive profile of emergence" (Avnimelech & Teubal, 2006, p. 1494). Moreover, Avnimelech et al. (2004) observed that the evolutionary processes were different. While the US VC emergence was market led,the Israeli VC emergence was policy driven. Lerner (2002) who believes external forces drive the cyclicality of VC markets urges policymakers to accelerate the cycles within the VC market by supporting trending technology classes in order to limit overinvestment in peak periods of the VC market which he calls overshooting. Overshooting makes investments inefficient and leads to disappointing returns and a countering effect of underinvestment in subsequent periods. However, due to the limited longitudinal research on the VC industry, the market indicators that determine when overshooting occurs is not well known. As Dodgson et al. (2008) suggest about research opportunities on evolution within innovation systems and the key constituents therein, there is an opportunity to explore innovation investment systems and forces within venture capital. The innovation system that is explored below is that of clean technology.

2.2.3 Cleantech Venture Capital

The cleantech investment category broadly includes investments in companies mitigating and adapting to climate change and encompasses several industry sectors. Research on venture capital in the cleantech space or some of its niches is rare. Prior research on the category depicts the characteristics and advantages but also challenges associated with cleantech and the VC industry. The following section overviews the scholarly work that involves the category and which played a significant role in shaping the discourse on cleantech investments.

Early work on VC and clean technologies opens the field by considering why so little capital had been invested in the sector and foresees a difficult future for the category (Diefendorf, 2000). Randjelovic, O'Rourke, and Orsato (2003) firstly mention the emergence of the cleantech category previously referred to as "environment-related VC" or "green VC". They define the investment category and show characteristics, processes and mechanisms as well as drivers and barriers in the field. They predicted that the category - then mostly supported through the idea of socially responsible investments (SRI) and an added ecological orientation - would become more mainstream in the future. "Continuing affirmation of the existence and importance of the sector has resulted in the acceptance of, and support for, the sector by established multinationals as well as governments." (Caprotti, 2012, p. 382). However, early levels of support, related technologies experience difficulties obtaining financing in this category due to policy preferences of investors in this field.

Wüstenhagen and Teppo (2006) revisit the emergence of the cleantech sector and looked at the perceived risk and expected return characteristics while also clarifying the path dependencies occurring within VC developments. They specifically call for research addressing "how new market sectors for VC investment emerge" (Wüstenhagen & Teppo, 2006, p. 81). O'Rourke (2009) examines the first decade (from 1995 to 2006) of the emergence of cleantech as an investment category. She describes the institutional processes of the emergence and creates a classification system for the category. Furthermore, she examines the investors which are active in the field and looks at their strategies. Caprotti (2012) analyses the development of the cleantech sector from a geographers standpoint over the period from 2000 to 2010. His work describes the sector through discursive logics as a socio-technical sector defined by a networks of actors. Three topics are core to the discourse: cleantech as a response to climate change, as a market opportunity and as a technological revolution.

Cleantech as a response to climate change. The social and ecological need for investments in renewable energies and clean technologies is stressed in a report for the

International Conference for Renewable Energies 2004. It emphasizes the role of VC to supply risk capital but foresees limited return possibilities in the highly risky sector (Sonntag-O'Brien & Usher, 2004).

Cleantech as a market opportunity. The few exit opportunities make it hard for investors to justify significant investments in risky clean energy technologies. Characteristics of path dependency are detected within the cleantech VC sector influencing investments in renewable energy and energy efficiency companies according to prevailing initial conditions (Marcus, Ellis, Malen, Drori, & Sened, 2011). A further work looks at the potential and limitations of VC for the clean energy sector. The authors analyze trends and draw the path to legitimization of the category. They raise several research questions for future scholars to pursue, one of them to research along the historical evolution of the category in a multisectoral way (Marcus et al., 2013). Bürer (2008) adds a policy angle on investment decisions and risk management practices within the clean energy private equity and VC sector. She explains the supportive nature of market-pull policies in favor of technology-push options and emphasizes the general importance of government actions to create market opportunity within this investment category.

Cleantech as a technological revolution. Ghosh and Nanda (2010) research on the role of VC for the commercialization of clean energy technologies. They focus on the problem of innovations associated with too much technology risk and at the same time requiring too much funding until maturity. Cleantech ventures are hard to fund and face the so called "Valley of Death". Establishing commercial viability for innovations already vetted and tested is difficult.

Kenney (2011b) is one sceptic concerning VC within the cleantech sector due to the lack of fit between traditional VC investment criteria and the characteristics of cleantech innovations. He suggests that in its current state, investments in cleantech would produce an unsustainable bubble. In contrast he advocates for investments in clean technologies that are more closely adapted to the traditional VC model and typical investment industries. For example, he suggests that investments in energy and efficiency software as well as smaller scale efficiency equipment are potential innovation paths. Another work that examines the fit of cleantech and VC considers the regulatory support mechanisms for the cleantech industry and criticizes the missing boundary conditions for a VC financed transformation through cleantech. Clean technology and in particular energy markets are generally large, however, they are not growing rapidly in most developed markets. The scalability of the highly capital intensive cleantech innovations due to production plants or material based processes is limited in comparison to many of the software based or biotech business models. Some exceptions might be technologies at the intersection between energy and the information technologies (Hargadon & Kenney, 2012). Otherwise, these conditions make it hard to find evidence for large and rapid value creation in cleantech markets. Therefore, in order to understand how new investment categories emerge, it is necessary to examine investment patterns in light of policy and market forces that hold the potential to influence investment decisions.

2.3 Research methodology & data

2.3.1 Data

This paper combines methodological approaches and datasets to provide a comprehensive picture of the historical emergence of VC investment in an emerging technology class. At the core is a database consisting of press publications from several major international newspapers which were compiled from January 1st 1995 to December 31st 2011. All articles from the selected newspapers during that time frame that mentioned the term "Venture Capital" were downloaded. The source of this data is Lexis Nexis which compiles international press. Within Lexis-Nexis, we chose the subset of "Major World Newspapers", which comprises 79 international newspapers in English language. This selection of articles makes it possible to analyze the development of the VC industry on a global level. In total there are 84,259 articles mentioning "Venture Capital" in the whole data set. The 17 years, which are observed, are divided into 68 quarters for the analysis. The lowest number of articles per quarter was published in the first quarter of 1995 with only 491 articles including "Venture Capital" appearing in major newspapers. The highest number of articles appeared in the second quarter of 2000 at 3097 articles.

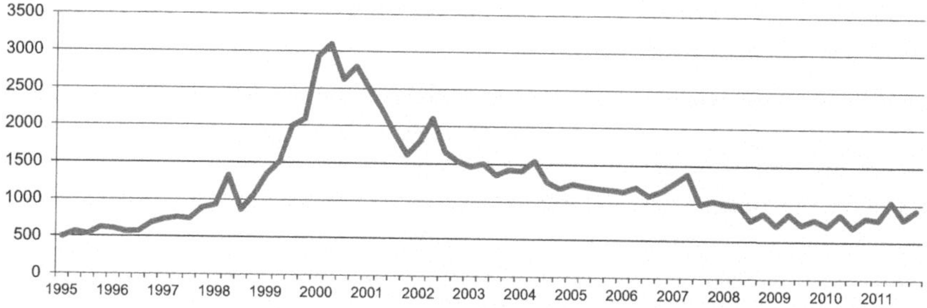

Figure 2 – Historical development of articles containing the term "Venture Capital"

The data resulting from the analysis of the media discourse is matched with investment data from the Thomson One Banker database of private equity investments. The investment data used is from the years 1995 until 2013. These data on total and subsector VC investments are from all global VC markets and include all investments from seed to late stage investments. Additionally, a comprehensive search for resources on the cleantech industry, (e.g. reports, policy papers and web media) was undertaken. These data have been thoroughly analyzed and used to confirm the findings of the other streams of research.

2.3.2 Method

This paper uses a quantitative content analysis of press articles to analyze and describe the case of the historical emergence and evolution of the cleantech investment category. Similar methods have found increasing prominence in organizational research recently (e.g. Phillips, Lawrence, & Hardy, 2004; Ventresca & Mohr, 2002; Wuthnow, 1989). For example, research on the historic shifting composition of actors and frames in corporate environmentalism (Hoffman, 1999) and the construction of market categories in the computer workstation market (Kennedy, 2005). McGrath (1998) used media patterns to analyze technology s-curves and technology cycles within the electric vehicle battery industry. Furthermore, the evolution of the U.S. satellite radio was researched over sixteen years based on a multitude of data sources including a large sample of newspaper articles. Within the textual documents changing thematic frames explained the differentiation in three different phases – emergence, commercialization, and early growth (Navis & Glynn, 2010). A further category emergence paper looks at the market for modern Indian art. A discourse analysis of diverse textual documents including newspaper articles shows the growing legitimization of the market category through a shared rhetoric (Khaire & Wadhwani, 2010).

The advantages of computer aided content analysis are in the depth of the assessment of a broad sample of textual documents (e.g. newspaper articles, excerpts). Additionally supporting is the independence from databases, which, especially in the field of VC investments, usually present a restricting factor in regard to data quality and availability. Resulting, quantitative content analysis enables a more detailed industry analysis than the assessment of classical venture databases (Berelson, 1952; Elo & Kyngäs, 2007; R. P. Weber, 1990). WordStat 6.0 by Provalis Research is a content analysis and text mining software for unstructured textual documents. It is used to analyze the created database based on a predefined dictionary, which is a collection of words, structured in several different subgroups. The software counts the words according to the structure defined in the dictionary (Krippendorff, 2012; Neuendorf, 2002).

As a foundation for structuring the cleantech sector dictionary, the taxonomy developed by the Cleantech Group2 was used. The Cleantech Group is one of the leading market intelligence companies in the field of clean technologies and is widely seen as influential over the establishment of the term "cleantech". The Cleantech Group's definition of the sector spans 13 categories encompassing several different industries and technologies. We built the dictionary according to these categories, and introduced two additional overview categories to observe general word groups related to "cleantech" and "ecology". These 15 different categories were applied to the quarterly structured articles from the 17 years from 1995 to 2011. The analyses permit us to give attention to included themes and technologies throughout the research period. Below, the relative importance of the cleantech category in entirety is contrasted to all VC mentioned. Specific sub-categories are reported in comparison to the cleantech category.

A description of the early years of the cleantech industry is found in O'Rourke (2009). Her analysis shows the important linkage of cleantech to the VC sector and defines it as a venture category. The analysis reports that 74% percent of all articles mentioning "cleantech" include mention of "venture capital". The analysis used in our study differs from O'Rourke (2009) - by looking at all articles mentioning "venture capital" and the terms associated with cleantech. "Greentech [Cleantech] VC investing has received little attention in the scholarly press, but enormous attention in the popular press" (Kenney, 2011b, p. 218). This paper modifies Venture Capital Life Cycle Model so far only used in a national context (Avnimelech et al., 2004; Avnimelech & Teubal, 2006).

To understand the detailed analysis of investment data this paper builds on the quantitative content analysis of a dataset of 84,259 articles reporting on "venture capital". Applying the assembled cleantech dictionary allows for fine-grained analysis of trending categories and themes at certain points in time. In order to investigate emergence it is necessary to have data predating emergence; for investment categories this implies the need to cover a time not observed by traditional financial databases or added to them post hoc (Woolley, 2011).

2 http://www.cleantech.com/

2.4 Results and discussion

2.4.1 The cleantech venture capital life cycle

The VC industry has experienced several booms and busts throughout its history. This pattern is of the form and character of a classical business cycle. The cycle whereby a new industry emerges with successful startups and good returns for VC funds to an industry with more funds being raised and bigger volumes leading to high competition for investments and high valuations and finally to the burst of the VC bubble. Despite its re-occurrence, industry and as well academia are often surprised each time the bubble bursts (Block & Sandner, 2009; Lerner, 2002; Mason, 2009). This pattern has appeared with changing amplitude in several countries, industries and investment stages (Lerner, 2002). The cyclicality and high volatility of the general VC market as well as the cleantech VC market can be observed in Figure 3. The Dotcom boom and crash of the late 1990s and early 2000s was an exceptionally high peak. The total VC market grew from $ 2.3 billion in the first quarter of 1995 to a peak of $ 43.7 billion in the second quarter 2000 just to drop to $ 9.1 billion less than three years later (Q1/2003).

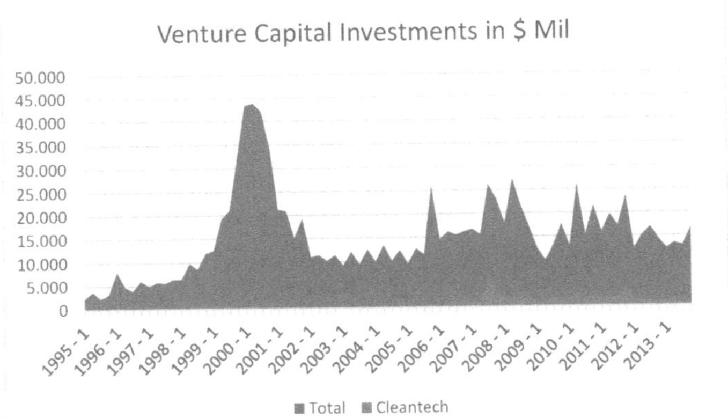

Figure 3 – Venture capital investments - total and cleantech from 1995 to 2013

The global media attention is aligned to the deals and investments as its pattern mirrors investment deals and it is highly correlated with the investments (see Table 2). While our data are not structured to inform us whether media or VC drives the conversation, it is clear that VC backed deals bring awareness of new technologies to mainstream media. This indicates that this media data can be used as a proxy for VC investment patterns.

	All Article	All Deal	All Invest	CT Article	CT Deal	CT Invest
All Article	1					
All Deal	0,78104389	1				
All Invest	0,6699168	0,91317293	1			
CT Article	-0,14846649	0,30272177	0,35815285	1		
CT Deal	-0,29431883	0,24240478	0,31221119	0,89394843	1	
CT Invest	-0,24197175	0,18057498	0,3423279	0,68266914	0,78225744	1

Table 2 – Correlation of VC general and CT – articles vs. investments

Figures 4 and 5 show the progression of total deals in the VC industry relative to the development of the total articles published on VC in the international newspapers, and the cleantech deals relative to the cleantech articles published in international newspapers. These charts suggest that media give less attention to VCs, except for when a new technology is being backed.

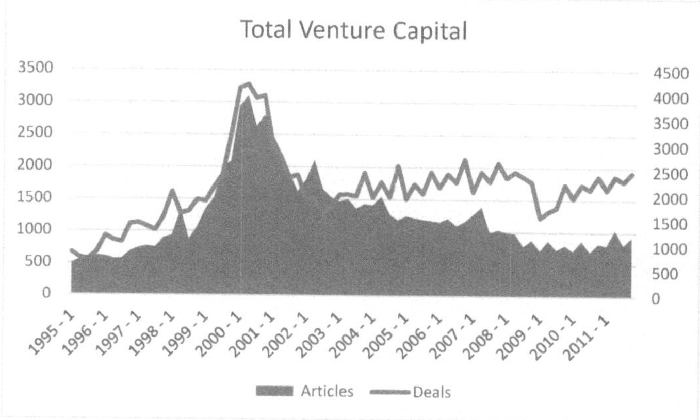

Figure 4 – Total venture capital articles and deals from 1995 to 2011

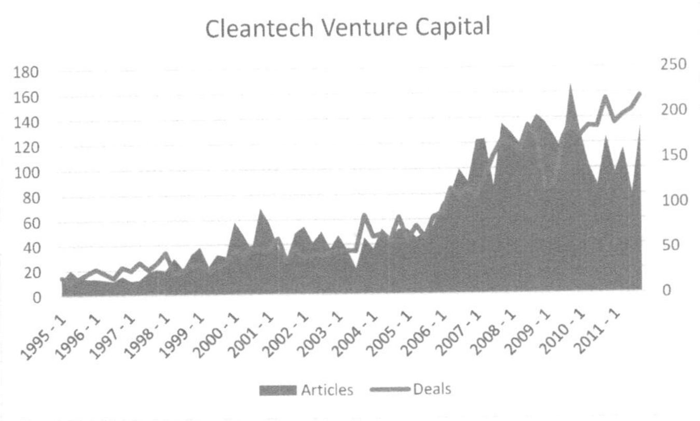

Figure 5 – Cleantech venture capital articles and deals from 1995 to 2011

From these general patterns of media on VC, we drill down further to understand the pattern of investments being made within the cleantech sector. Figure 6 displays the results of the quantitative content analysis. Applying the cleantech dictionary to the media database[3], we see that media attention differed across quarters and/or years, permitting us to determine the relative importance of various technologies in different time periods, which we have organized into life cycle stages.

3 The "Air" theme as part of the taxonomy has proved to include too many articles not properly fitting the categorization so this theme has been left out for the analysis.

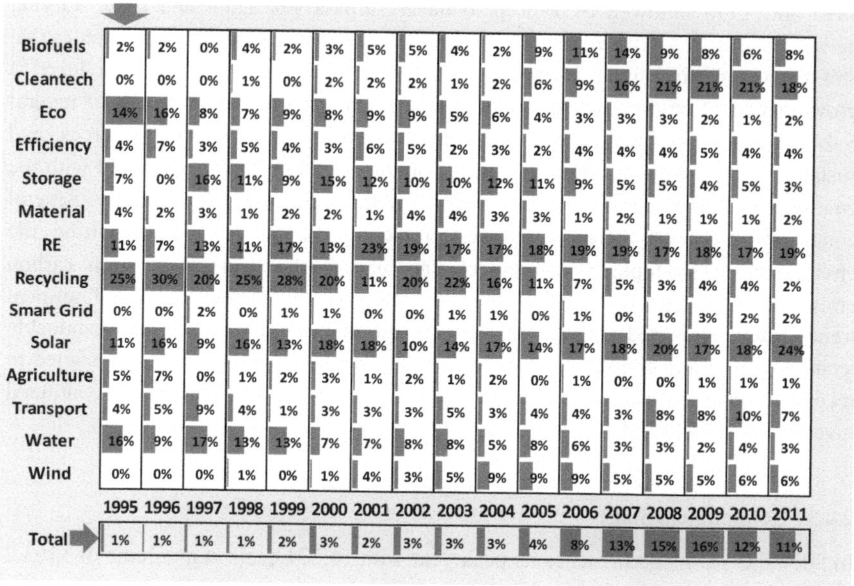

Figure 6 – Dictionary application – sector importance in venture capital articles

2.4.2 Early Investment Stage

In 1995, less than 1.5% of the $11.4 billion VC deals went to cleantech companies (78 deals, $168 million). Media attention, by comparison, is slightly higher at 2.7% discourse on cleantech related issues. By 1998, the VC market grew to $36.5 billion (7317 deals), however, the share of cleantech investments fell to .7%, or $269 million invested in 163 deals, and media attention dropped to 2.4%. Recycling is the dominant category in the media in this phase. It is one of the categories usually connected with environmentalism. The amount of articles within the relevant cleantech frame mentioning this theme fluctuates between 20 and 30%. Other themes mentioned more often are water, between 9 and 17%, ecology, with 14 and 16% in 1995 and 1996 followed by a drop to never surpass 9% again and solar, varying between 9 and 16%.

In this stage, recycling is the dominant category in the media. It is one of the categories commonly connected with environmentalism. The volume of articles relevant mentioning this theme fluctuates between 20 and 30%. Other themes mentioned more often are water, between 9 and 17%, ecology, with 14 and 16% in

1995 and 1996 followed by a drop to never surpass 9% again and solar, varying between 9 and 16%. These themes reflect VC investments in cleantech companies that are responding to climate change. The late 1980s and early 1990s introduced a growing fear of environmental pollution and recognition of the finiteness of natural resources, and heightened consciousness concerning the use of resources and sustainable consumption. The growing importance of these topics, combined with the emergence of green parties lead to political initiatives for more sustainability. Several countries introduced different policies protecting the nature and supporting the environment. The topic of climate change lead to the decision to limit carbon emissions at the United Nations conference in Kyoto 1997. These social and political trends were supported through the investment into more research on sustainable technologies at universities and corporations. As a result, startups and SME started to recognize opportunities in the cleantech context as well, which fostered the continued investments in cleantech.

2.4.3 Commitment Stage

In 2000 the VC market reaches its peak year with 16,279 deals at a volume of $163.2 billion. Approximately 0.8% of the total deal volume went to 193 cleantech deals, totalling $1.2 billion. This investment represents a significant rise in absolute terms and as well as in average deal size. Media attention hovers around 1.8% of cleantech articles. After the Dotcom crash, the total VC market drops to $ 42.9 billion invested in 8516 deals in 2003. However, Cleantech investments drop not nearly as much with $916 million invested in 232 deals. This investment represented 2.1% of all money invested and an increase relative to other years. The media attention for cleantech rose to 2.6% as well.

Recycling remains an important media topic. Water and Ecology lose their importance while solar as a media topic increases to 18% as it wins economic importance at the same time. During this phase wind is mentioned significantly more often starting in 2001 but still only reaches maximal 5% of the attention in 2003. Energy storage especially fuel cells are an important topic of the early 2000s which shows through higher media attention of around 10 to 15%. Attention towards other renewables raises to around 20% or higher.

These investments reflect increasing commitment to cleantech. In the earliest years of the commitment stage the VC market reached levels never seen before in terms of money invested and average valuations. The positive environment for VC investments promoted growth in nearly every part of the industry. Cleantech deals were happening more frequently even though they were not yet called cleantech or even grouped into a category. Well regarded VCs like Venrock Associates, 3i Group and Draper Fisher Jurvetson made their initial investments in what would later be categorized as cleantech in 2001/2002. Early dedicated funds like the SAM Private Equity Energy Fund closed in 2000, while SAIL Capital Partners closed their first fund in 2002. At the same time technological breakthroughs happen in the renewable energy and fuel cell industry which steer attention towards the possibilities in the category. Entrepreneurial activity is also rising with startups that become role models for getting funded in that period. Tesla Motors for example, which was incorporated in July 2003 was later financed with several hundred million dollars of VC money before it went public. These facts demonstrate that cleantech had become viewed as a clear market opportunity.

2.4.4 Institutionalization Stage

By 2004, VC has slightly recovered with 8,840 deals at a volume of $45.5 billion. Nearly 3% of the total deal volume was spent on 277 cleantech deals, totaling $1.3 billion. Media attention to cleantech articles rises to 3.4 %. In 2007, when cleantech had its peak year the global VC industry invested $ 81.3 billion in 9,525 deals and within the cleantech category it invested $ 12.4 billion in 561 deals which is 15.3% of the whole market. Media attention towards cleantech was also high at 10%.

In 2005 the cleantech category was growing immensely in media attention. The relative importance for all cleantech associated articles jumps from 2% in 2004 to 9% in 2005. Mainstream media incorporated the terminology relatively late. From the mid-1990's more specialized media reported on the category frequently. Therefore, the category had reached some legitimacy even outside of the VC industry by 2005 (O'Rourke, 2009). In the institutionlization stage the relative importance of recycling disappears. Media attention drops to 11% in 2005 followed by a steady decline down to 2 to 4% until the end time period. This drastic shift away from technologies focused on addressing climate change to other technology categories shows the closeness of the category to market driven businesses as discussed by Caprotti (2012). Wind, Solar and other Renewable Energy Sources reached their maximal importance during the institutionalization stage. Wind peaks at 9% from 2004 to 2006, solar fluctuates between 14 and 20%, and other renewables stay at 17 to 19%. Additionally there is a brief increase in attention towards biofuels, which appear more heavily in 2005 with 9% of the attention and rises to 14% in 2007.

The cleantech VC category is firmly established in the institutionalization stage. With the burst of the Dotcom bubble, mainstream VC investors sought new investment areas. Combined with the attacks on the World Trade Center in New York City, there was increased interest in reducing dependence on oil-based technologies. Another major turning point for cleantech investment was California's Green Wave initiative. Beginning in early 2004 the treasurer of California mandated CalPERS and CalSTRS to invest into environmental conscious assets. The first $500 million tranche was earmarked for PE/VC investments to develop clean technologies. This public effort spearheaded the widespread acceptance of the category and influenced many of the developments of the category. There was a clear shift towards cleantech for technological revolution.

These factors motivated VC investors to consider industries which, by mid-2004 were labeled as cleantech, as a suitable investment field. As a result, cleantech VC investments category expanded rapidly. With dedicated funds, mandates arise from pension funds or corporate investors and big multi fund investors seeking to raise new fund vehicles targeted at the cleantech market. KPCB for example launched their Green Growth fund in early 2008. The support for cleantech is changing drastically as well. For example, in 2004 Germany's "Renewable Energy Sources Act" drove installations of RE technologies. The solar energy market grew immensely during this time, even though it has not been economically viable without public support. This rise in demand led to more and more company formations in the RE and solar fields worldwide.

Relevance as an investment category creates a VC and entrepreneurial network co-evolution process. The popularity of cleantech across investment participants, from institutional investors over VC funds to start-ups fosters a growing market. A general understanding of industry participants and technologies exists (Caprotti, 2012; O'Rourke, 2009). Market information/ support providers like the Cleantech Group, Clean Edge, and New Energy Finance gain importance and provide databases, reports and organize conferences and fairs to promote the industry (see O'Rourke, 2009 for a detailed analysis on cleantech service providers). High growth attracts general VCs without prior experience in asset heavy industries like cleantech start entering the category and results in new and less skilled VC managers raising funds. The abundance of capital spread across companies, and leads to increased competition, high valuations and skepticism about the long term viability of funded companies. This later stage introduces overshooting (Lerner, 2002).

2.4.5 Overshooting Stage

The volume of the VC market dropped drastically after Q4/2008. In 2009 the VCs invested only $ 53 billion in 7,279 deals. Within the cleantech category less than half of the prior year's total - $ 5.2 billion was invested in 598 deals. At this level, the average deal size plummeted by more than 60% compared to the peak year 2007. Nevertheless media attention for cleantech reached its peak in 2009 with a share of 17.4%. However, largely due to press regarding bankruptcies of cleantech firms and the failure of stimulus programs like the DOE-LGP.

In late 2008 and early 2009 media use of the term Cleantech reached its peak. 21% of all articles of the cleantech frame mention that specific topic. Further dominant topics in media are Other RE and Solar with 18 and 17% of the attention. For the first time the topic Smart Grid gains some relevant attention and reaches 3% of media discourse. This announces the change towards less asset heavy investment categories within the cleantech category. The transportation topic which has some more attention as well is supporting this trend but has some link to the stimulus packages for large VC financed companies like Tesla Motors or Fisker Automotive.

The burst of the US housing bubble and the loss of trust in many financial institutions led to the beginning of a global recession. The confidence in the markets had to be supported by heavy government actions to save the financial system, especially US banks and insurance companies. On September 15, 2008, the bankruptcy of Lehman Brothers was announced and the financial crisis became apparent. This recession hit the VC markets as well.

Governments around the world introduced stimulus programs to support recovery most often with a focus on green growth, examples include the ARPA-E in the USA and the Green New Deal Package in Korea (UNEP, 2009). These initiatives strengthened the cleantech category. Concurrently, policymakers started several initiatives to "de-risk" capital markets through new regulation like Basel III or Solvency II[4]. Over time these policies decreased allocations towards riskier assets like cleantech VC.

4 Basel III and Solvency II are comprehensive reform measures to strengthen the regulation, supervision and risk management of banks or respectively insurance companies. Core initiatives include increasing capital & liquidity requirements and higher risk discipline in investments.

2.4.6 Stabilization Stage

Following overshooting, the cleantech VC category consolidated and restructured. Investment volumes regained $2 billion in Q1/2010: New company formations like Nest Labs, a developer and manufacturer of smart thermostats which was founded in 2010, financed by major VCs and sold to Google in early 2014 for $ 3.2 billion in cash. Tesla Motors the manufacturer of electric cars founded in 2003 went public in Q2/2010. Exits and IPOs restored confidence in the category. Even struggling companies like Fisker Automotive another car manufacturer or A123 a battery manufacturer who went into bankruptcy in 2013 were saved and are still active under new ownership.

The overall VC industry recovered in 2010 and 2011 to reach $ 76.3 billion invested in 9,307 deals. The cleantech category reached almost $ 9 billion invested in 806 deals for a share at 11.7%. Still in the following years the total VC market consolidated and lost some ground. In 2013 just $ 55.3 billion were invested in 512 deals with $ 3.4 billion invested in 512 cleantech deals. This reflects a change in the investment category to technologies that are both less expensive to bring to maturity and less asset heavy.

Technologies such as transportation and smart grid received increased media attention beginning in late 2009. Wind and Solar which had reached widespread market adoption are still of very high importance in media discourse. Nonetheless investors are hesitant to invest in asset intensive companies and focus on less capital intensive companies with a software or consumer focused market (Hargadon & Kenney, 2012; Kenney, 2011b). In general newly founded startups in this stage are market driven rather than policy dependent. Thus, markets with reliable market-pull regulation may benefit from new company foundations, as policies align with the VC approach better than technology push policies (Mary Jean Bürer & Wüstenhagen, 2009).

We summarize each of these life cycle stages in a comprehensive manner in Table 3. The structure stems from previous work (Avnimelech et al., 2004; Avnimelech & Teubal, 2006) and has been refined for the category emergence analysis.

	Hightech VC categories	Cleantech VC category
		Length of pre-emergence and emergence phases-8 years *VC emergence - first policy led now market led*
Background Conditions Phase	• Market need • Political initiatives • Creation of industry R&D/innovation capabilities in university labs and corporates • Startups and SME recognize opportunities	• Fear of environmental pollution and finiteness of natural resources • Political initiatives for more sustainability • Creation of cleantech R&D/innovation capabilities in university labs and corporates • Startups and SME recognize opportunities in cleantech context
Pre-Emergence Phase	• Technological breakthroughs/revolution • Growth of VC in general and first investments in category area by general funds • Increasing numbers of startups excess demand for VC investments	• Solar energy, wind energy and energy efficiency technologies enter the market • First investments in cleantech by general funds • Innovators start cleantech companies and are looking for funding
Emergence Phase	• High rate of growth of VC and founding activity • VC-SU co-evolution process; strong collective and onset of cumulative process • Increased competition and overshooting • Entry of less skilled VC managers/firms and startup companies	• First dedicated cleantech funds start operations • Support environment through databases (Cleantech Group/New Energy Finance) and specialized service firms grows • High competition and therefore high valuations for top deals • Several new and established VC firms open clean/green/sustainable fund
Crisis Phase	• A deep crisis that may be caused by a one or combination of factors including stock market downturn causing an inability to have IPO (sometimes termed "overshooting," • Negative government actions, more general economic downturn, etc. • Exit of VC funds and closure of SUs, while SUs suffer liquidity problems General loss of confidence in the industry	• Financial crisis started by US housing bubble & Lehman Brothers bankruptcy • Governments "de-risk" capital markets through new regulation • Unfavorable returns lead to drying fundraising conditions especially in the young cleantech field
Consolidation Phase	• The VC industry restructures with the help of collective institutions • New institutions (formal and informal) emerge • New government policies are implemented	• New growth in less policy driven markets • Market pull for technologies and following investments - less asset heavy and faster to maturity • Returning confidence through first exits

Table 3 – Description of life cycle phases

2.5 Conclusion

This research aimed to understand VC investment patterns in an emerging technology sector. We examined the emerging cleantech sector and considered the evolutionary influences in the early and expansion stages of the life cycle of the adjoining investment category. The results clearly reflect that VC investment patterns occurred in stages, beginning with early investments and proceeding through commitment and institutionalization stages where the technology class becomes more accepted. Investments during these times align with broader societal trends in this whether the technology responded to climate change, represented a clear market opportunity in the sector and then finally those that represented a technological revolution for the category. They illustrate that investments begin slow and at small amounts, perhaps to provide low-cost learning opportunities to the involved VCs, and then increase in amount and volume over time. Also observed was an overshooting stage where VC investors investments capped out and began to slow, and finally a stabilization stage where investments were diverted into specific types of investments in order to capture value in VC investments. Overall, these results strongly support the work of Caprotti (2012) and Ghosh and Nanda (2010).

This paper provides insights into the evolution of cleantech financing. The joint analysis of press publications and investment data highlights understanding of historical turning points in the sector. A variety of factors such as policy changes, political shifts in direction, investment programs and global trends or phenomena likely underlie these investment patterns and influence market growth and public perception. Deeper knowledge of these factors would enhance understanding of emerging investment categories. The understanding can support in the construction of public measures or supporting frameworks to foster innovation and job creation in desired industries. This paper contributes to different streams of literature, first on the historical emergence of VC investments and second, on the role of VCs in industry development. Additionally we advance the literature on cleantech and sustainable VC (Caprotti, 2012; O'Rourke, 2009; Pernick & Wilder, 2007). Finally, we make a methodological contribution by showing the usefulness of media data as a proxy for VC investments.

The approach used in this paper is one of the few examples of a conceptualized framework for the historical analysis of a VC market (Avnimelech et al., 2004; Avnimelech & Teubal, 2006). It transferred a life cycle model from the national to an industry level and introduced methodology to interpret the changing themes within the VC industry. The VC life cycle model aims to understand the establishment of the cleantech VC category and its environment.. VCs changed the look of the category and ultimately pushed the market towards a dominant design (von Burg & Kenney, 2000). By leveraging the growing environmentalism of the late 1980s and early 1990s and political initiative to support sustainability, VCs were able to help finance an emerging industry. Moreover, through market pull, for example through Germany's renewable energy feed-in-tariff and on the other hand, and direct investment support like California's Green Wave initiative, the cleantech category was poised for investment. However, the policy driven support led to an immense growth and "overshooting" (Lerner, 2002) which in addition to the financial crisis reversed the momentum the industry had been experiencing.

Our results call for for thoughtful use of policy instruments in emerging industry contexts as too much policy stimulation can saturate the market. A consistent and reliable regulatory environment that encourages technology-push policies in earlier stages and market-pull policies in later stages with a relatively free acting and without overshooting the financial system would contribute to sustainable industries that not only provide impressive returns for investors but also contributes to sustainable economic growth and job creation. While we believe the combined analysis of the emerging VC investment category for clean teach emergence should transfer to other industries and investment category contexts, we encourage research that validates this assumption. The quantative content analysis can be biased based on the dictionary development and depends upon predefined textual information (Hsieh & Shannon, 2005). Therefore, testing our findings through different quantitative analysis could enrich the overall contribution and strengthen knowledge transferability.

2.6 Acknowledgements

The authors are grateful for the time and support of Martin Kenney, Ramana Nanda, Dimo Dimov and Gavin Cassar as well as anonymous conference reviewers for valuable comments on earlier versions of the paper. The opportunity to present and discuss earlier versions of the paper at SEE Conference 2012 in Denver, RENT Conference 2012 in Lyon and at the ISPIM Symposium 2012 in Seoul helped us tremendously in further refining our argument.

The research team would like to thank the Federal Ministry of Education and Research (BMBF), Germany, for their financial support as part of the research project ''Climate Change, Financial Markets and Innovation (CFI)''.

3 Private Equity in Clean Technology: An Exploratory Study of the Finance-Innovation-Policy Nexus

Authors: Michael Migendt, Florian Schock, Florian A. Täube, Paschen von Flotow & Friedemann Polzin,

Abstract:

The role of technological innovation in mitigating climate change has received growing interest in recent years. However, extant literature has neglected a more holistic view on equity financing and the indirect effects of innovation and financial policy on financing innovation through private equity (PE) and venture capital (VC). In this paper, we emphasize the importance of this understudied aspect through a comparative case study of private equity and venture capital for clean technologies in the United States and Germany. We find that systemic interdependencies between institutional investors, PE/ VC and policy makers influence the conditions for innovation – the "finance-innovation-policy nexus". Adverse effects of policies affecting financial markets, in particular institutional investors, have to be taken into account to effectively mobilize private investments for (cleantech) innovation.

3.1 Introduction

The role of technological innovation, particularly in mitigating climate change has received growing interest in recent years (Arora, Romijn, & Caniëls, 2014; Mingo & Khanna, 2014; Mowery et al., 2010a). In order to achieve a transition to a more sustainable economy, scholars have argued that at least part of the necessary innovations have to come from entrepreneurial ventures rather than large corporations (Garud & Karnøe, 2003; Hockerts & Wüstenhagen, 2010b; Sine & David, 2003). This leads to two fundamental and interlinked challenges for the transition towards a low-carbon economy.

First, the single biggest problem for these entrepreneurial firms is access to finance (Lerner, 2002; Mina et al., 2013; Schneider & Veugelers, 2010; Stucki, 2014). Although recent changes in monetary policy by central banks have led to low interest rates and heavy injections of liquidity into financial markets (Belke, 2013), investments into innovative companies and in key enabling technologies for a sustainability transition (clean technologies, nano technologies and biotech) have only recently seen a slight recovery (McCrone, 2015). The drastic change in the investment landscape for cleantech can be observed through the continuous downturn in investments following the financial crisis of 2008. This change is particularly visible in early stage VC where the investment market almost disappeared (see Figure 7).

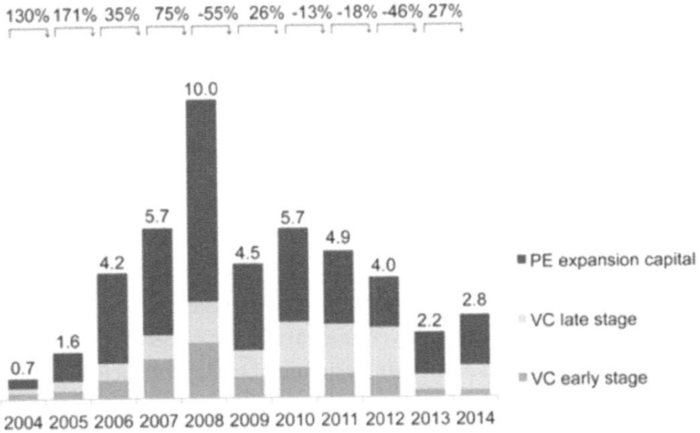

Figure 7 – Global VC/PE investment in CT by stage in USD bn (Source: McCrone, (2015))

Second, cleantech ventures exhibit specific characteristics, such as higher policy risk, asset-heaviness, slower scalability and corresponding long payback periods which have to be addressed differently by policy makers compared to other high-tech industries (Hargadon & Kenney, 2012; Hockerts & Wüstenhagen, 2010b; Petkova, Wadhwa, Yao, & Jain, 2014). The literature on policy measures to stimulate innovation demonstrates that certain cleantech industries would not exist without market-pull regulations, such as the feed-in tariff (U. C. Haley & Schuler, 2011; Veugelers, 2012a; Polzin, Migendt, Täube, & von Flotow, 2015; Wüstenhagen & Bilharz, 2006a).

Despite the importance of innovation by entrepreneurial ventures and the dependence on access to funding, there is little research that addresses the role of entrepreneurial finance *in a larger picture*, let alone the impact of policy (for an overview, see O'Sullivan, 2005; Hirsch-Kreinsen, 2011; Perez, 2002b). Most of this literature (also with regard to the cleantech focus) is limited to an analysis of the VC-entrepreneur relationship (Dimov, Holan, & Milanov, 2012; Kenney, 2011b; Petkova et al., 2014) and the policy-VC relationship (Bottazzi & Da Rin, 2002; Kortum & Lerner, 2000a; Lerner & Tåg, 2013a). Yet, the source of funds that propels VC – institutional investors - is rarely studied by innovation scholars. Overall, equity finance for innovation has not been analyzed as an independent, let alone central element in the innovation-policy-nexus (for cleantech) (Kenney, 2011a; Mazzucato, 2013a; Wonglimpiyarat, 2011; Lerner, 2002, 2009).

Thus our research question reads as follows: *How does the interplay between equity finance and corresponding policy measures influence (cleantech) innovation and entrepreneurship?*

In this paper, we emphasize the importance of this hitherto-neglected role of finance for clean technologies (Cleantech, or CT) comparing the United States and Germany. We contribute to the literature through a comprehensive qualitative analysis of the policy-finance-innovation interdependencies and relationships by explicitly incorporating the financial sector, namely institutional investors. While innovation policy might try to foster financing of start-ups through certain innovation policy measures aimed at venture capital (VC) investors and private equity (PE), regulatory requirements in other subsectors, such as institutional investors, can counterweigh these positive effects. This stems from the fact that VC/PE investors refrain from risky investments into early stage technology ventures as a result of regulatory tightening of their own sources, namely institutional investors. We conclude with implications for theory and practice.

3.2 Theoretical Background

3.2.1 Role of the finance eco-system for innovation

One of the most relevant problems, not only after, but aggravated through the financial crises, has been the mobilization of finance for (cleantech) innovation in firms (Mathews et al., 2010a; Mazzucato, 2013a; Mina et al., 2013; Stucki, 2014). Yet, the literature has neglected a holistic view on the role of equity finance in innovation, although it is regarded as a critical component and crucial for entrepreneurship and market creation (Dosi, 1990; Mazzucato, 2013a, 2013b; O'Sullivan, 2005; Perez, 2002b). The main participants in the finance-innovation-ecosystem are shown in Table 4.

Term	Definition	Sources
Cleantech (companies)	Technologies that focus on sustainability, mitigation and adaptation to climate change, or reduction of natural resources. For example, solar or wind energy technologies, electric cars, energy efficiency technologies and other smart resource reduction approaches.	(Caprotti, 2012; O'Rourke, 2009; Pernick & Wilder, 2007)
Venture Capital (VC)	Early-stage and growth equity capital with a high risk/return profile.	(Bottazzi & Rin, 2002; Dimov et al., 2012; Kortum & Lerner, 2000b; Oakey, 2003)
Private Equity (PE)	Late-stage/ expansion/ turnaround equity capital, lower risk/return profile.	(Lerner, Sorensen, & Strömberg, 2011; Schock, 2014; Wright, Gilligan, & Amess, 2009; Wright & Robbie, 1998)
Institutional Investors	Investment and pension funds, banks and insurance companies) are strategic equity investors that look for a long-term investment and stable returns.	(Brossard, Lavigne, & Sakinç, 2013b; OECD, 2013b)
Policy makers	Employees of ministries, government representatives, institutional intermediaries that create/deploy innovation policy and financial regulation and thus shape market conditions.	(Marry Jean Bürer & Wüstenhagen, 2009; Hoppmann, Peters, Schneider, & Hoffmann, 2013; Peters, Schneider, Griesshaber, & Hoffmann, 2012b; Polzin, von Flotow, & Klerkx, 2016)

Table 4 – Key actors in the finance-innovation eco-system (definitions)

On a macro-level most of the literature found a positive impact of VC/PE on technological change, innovation, industry evolution or economic growth (Avnimelech & Teubal, 2006; Bottazzi & Da Rin, 2002; Florida & Kenney, 1988b; Kortum & Lerner, 2000a; Mina et al., 2013; Samila & Sorenson, 2010b). However VC is only suitable for a small number of high-growth firms (Hargadon & Kenney, 2012; Kenney, 2011a). On the micro-level scholars analyzed the decision making of venture capitalists in emerging industries or more general the VC/PE-innovator relationship (Dimov et al., 2012; Petkova et al., 2014). A similar picture can be drawn when looking at research that has analyzed alternative investments such as VC in clean technology industries. So far scholars looked at the emergence of those investors and their contribution to low-carbon innovation (Ghosh & Nanda, 2010; Marcus et al., 2013; Randjelovic et al., 2003) also pointing out some limitations of the VC business model and perceived challenges for sustainability-oriented VC (Bocken, 2015; Kenney, 2011b; Nanda, Younge, & Fleming, 2014). These challenges comprise a high technological uncertainty, regulatory dependency, asset-heaviness and difficult scalability (Foxon & Pearson, 2008a; Polzin et al., 2016).

There are few scholarly exceptions that analyse equity finance for innovation in a larger picture (Avnimelech & Teubal, 2006; Brossard et al., 2013a; Grilli & Murtinu, 2014; Kenney, 2011b; Oakey, 2003; Revest & Sapio, 2013; Wonglimpiyarat, 2011). This stream of literature considers the importance of institutional investors for innovation on a firm level and for industry emergence. However they do not assess the relation between institutional investors and VC/PE and eventually investments into (cleantech) ventures. Surprising in terms of theory alone, the relevance of this gap increases further because of the repercussions of the financial and economic crisis, which include the tightening regulation of financial markets largely affecting institutional investors.

3.2.2 Public policy influence on the finance-innovation relationship

In order to mobilize private equity funds, policy makers possess a set of instruments, ranging from regulation, economic and voluntary instruments that are part of a 'policy mix' (Borrás & Edquist, 2013; Flanagan, Uyarra, & Laranja, 2011b; Magro & Wilson, 2013; Mathews et al., 2010a; Veugelers, 2012a). An overview about the policy measures discussed in this article can be drawn from Table 5. On the one hand public policy is considered a main driver for market development as it adjusts institutions and supports specific sectors by using technology-push and demand-pull mechanisms (Criscuolo & Menon, 2015; Hoppmann et al., 2013; Olmos, Ruester, & Liong, 2012; Polzin et al., 2015; Tsoutsos & Stamboulis, 2005). Olmos et al. (2012) discuss policy measures and financing instruments to induce cleantech innovation, highlighting subsidies, loans, equity investments and tax-credits as suitable. Hoppmann et al. (2013) particularly argue that deployment policies leads to a shift of investments in companies to pursue more mature technological trajectories limiting their investments in novel explorations ('investor effect') which is valued by VC investors (Mary Jean Bürer & Wüstenhagen, 2009). Finally Veugelers (2012a) and Chrisculo & Menon (2015) find that deployment measures focusing on the long-term are conducive to innovation and VC investments in cleantech. This corresponds with research into policy implementation which highlights regulatory uncertainty and policy risk appear as major barriers (Lüthi & Wüstenhagen, 2012a; Marcus, Aragon-Correa, & Pinkse, 2011).

Type of policy	Sources	United States (Examples discussed in this paper)	Germany (Examples discussed in this paper)
Innovation policy (Market pull)	(Marry Jean Bürer & Wüstenhagen, 2009; U. C. V. Haley & Schuler, 2011; Hoppmann et al., 2013; Peters et al., 2012b)	Cash rebates, direct investments, Loan guarantee program (LGP), subsidies,	Tax incentives, Feed-in tariffs, subsidies, Public (institutional) investments
Innovation policy (Technology-push)	(Marry Jean Bürer & Wüstenhagen, 2009; Olmos et al., 2012; Wüstenhagen & Bilharz, 2006b)	R&D support, subsidies, tax credits	R&D support, subsidies, tax credits
Regulation (Innovation)	(Bottazzi & Rin, 2002; Da Rin, Nicodano, & Sembenelli, 2006b; Lerner & Tåg, 2013b)	Calpers/Calsters (Pension fund mandates)	VC policy framework (general conditions)
Regulation (Financial markets)	*Not discussed in the relation to (cleantech) innovation*	AIFM, Dodd-Frank-Act, Volcker rule	Basel III, Solvency II, AIFM

Table 5 – Overview of policy measures discussed

On the other hand prior research on the complex interactions between financial markets, innovation policy and innovation has focused on the VC-policy relationship (Bottazzi & Da Rin, 2002; Da Rin et al., 2006b; Lerner & Tåg, 2013a). These studies compare European and US VC markets, highlighting favourable policy measures for creating VC markets such as adjustments of capital gains tax and capital market development (Bottazzi & Da Rin, 2002; Da Rin et al., 2006b). Lerner (2002, 2009) finds that in the US while designing supportive VC environments, policy makers lack an understanding of the entrepreneurial and investments process and criteria being used by investors. Recently, Lerner & Tåg (2013a) compared the VC financing systems of the US and Sweden, highlighting key institutions such as the legal environment, financial market development, taxation, labor market regulations, and public R&D spending as most relevant for the creation of active venture capital markets. One of their findings relates a thriving VC industry to exit opportunities in developed financial markets. They also found positive influence of deregulation, e.g.

allowing pension funds to invest in VC (Gompers & Lerner, 2001). However, tightening regulation has not been studied as an influencing factor for PE investments (Lerner & Tåg, 2013a).

We bridge two streams of literature that looked at the relationship between VC/PE and the influence of policies on VC/PE investments (in the cleantech sphere). From a systemic perspective, innovation in clean technologies is influenced not only by innovation-oriented policies but also by financial policies targeting other actors in the financial markets through interdependdencies (see also the discussion of systemic problems by Edquist, 2011; and K. M. Weber & Rohracher, 2012). We therefore emphasize the role of equity finance and financial regulation of institutional investors. Accordingly, financial policy potentially has an impact on innovation outcomes. In this paper, we investigate systemic by focusing on direct and indirect effects of financial policy and innovation-oriented policies in the CT area in a cross-country comparison. Our stylized theoretical model that depicts the main actors and relationships in the equity-ecosystem for financing (cleantech) innovation can be drawn from Figure 8.

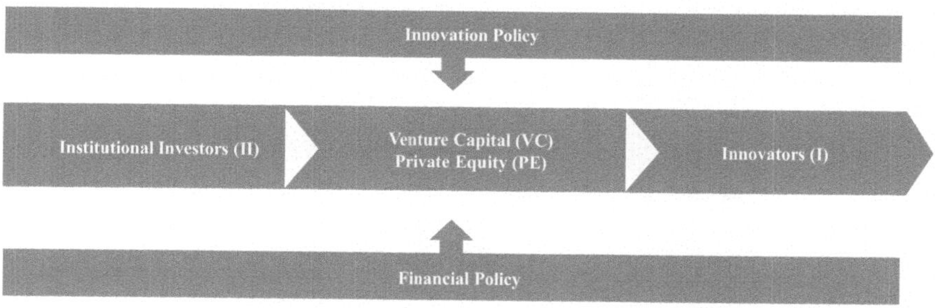

Figure 8 – Theoretical framework

3.3 Method and Data

In order to understand and analyze the interactions between policy and equity finance for (cleantech) innovation, we use a qualitative research approach. Our research covers the clean technology (CT) area, especially in the field of innovative companies funded by VC/PE capital or requiring external equity capital. These kinds of investments often are not publicly announced or tracked. Hence there is a scarcity of data, especially in emerging fields. Qualitative research approaches help to overcome the burden of insufficient available data and complex research settings including multiple actors and interdependencies (K. M. Eisenhardt, 1989; Yin, 2009). The cases Germany and the US have been chosen to illustrate the effects of different state and structure of equity markets on innovation activities in two relevant cleantech markets.

3.3.1 Research Context

The cleantech sector has been growing rapidly which can be seen from the financial flows into the different CT asset classes (Figure 9)[5]. Starting from the early 2000s it was experiencing a boom, with rapid growth until the financial crisis in 2008. This slowed down the development only to recover shortly thereafter with a continuing growth, notably in asset finance and new electricity generating capacity (Ettenhuber, 2013; PwC Moneytree, 2014).

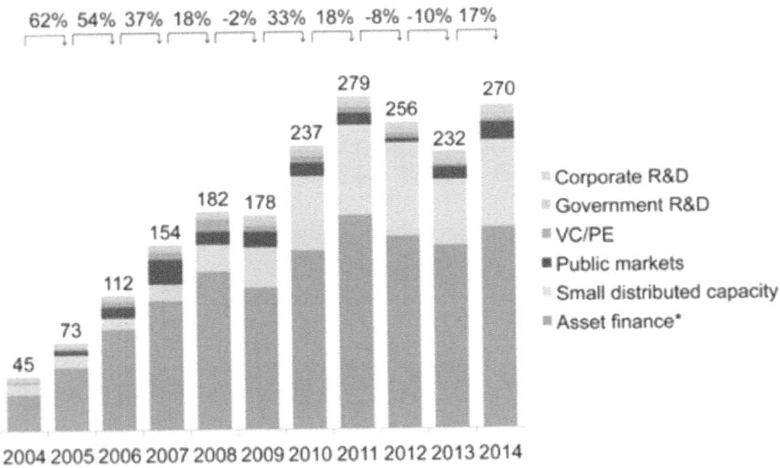

Figure 9 – Global new investment in CT in USD bn

5 Here we use the investments in clean/renewable energy technologies as a proxy for investments for clean technologies in general. BNEF provides the most comprehensive database concerning different asset classes for clean technologies (i.e. Asset finance, VC/PE, Mergers&Acquisitions, Public Equity, Corporate debt, etc.). Similar trends can be observed in broader databases such as Thomson Reuters (PwC Moneytree, 2014, 2015)

The financial crisis, consisting of a housing bubble in the United States, bank insolvencies and national financial and economic turmoil was responded to with recovery policies for industry and restrictive financial policies in the US and Europe alike. On the financial side, these measures include Basel III[6], Solvency II[7], the Dodd-Frank Act[8], and the Volcker rule[9]. On the industrial side, there was an unprecedented surge of government R&D and grant capital commitments to the CT sector which coincided with the shrinking bank-lending and VC/PE activities throughout the US, Europe and Germany in particular (see Figure 10). This highly supportive public environment for cleantech innovation aimed at maintaining economic stability and at accelerating growth while assisting efforts towards sustainability transition with measures such as cash rebates, direct investments, loan guarantee programs, feed-in tariffs and R&D support. Even though the CT sector, especially the deployment of technologies was supported, investment activity in the US and Germany declined over the years as can be observed (see Figure 10). After a continuous growth the numbers show a drastic decline 2010-2012. With regard to VC investments a slight recovery on a lower level is visible for the US. Investments in Germany on the other hand could achieve the level of 2005-2007. In 2014 the graphs show a steep recovery for PE investments in the US whereas in Germany a weaker recovery is visible.

---

6 Basel III is a comprehensive set of reform measures to strengthen the regulation, supervision and risk management of banks. It includes several pillars which increase capital & liquidity requirements and demand more risk discipline (Bank for International Settlements, 2010).

7 The Solvency I and II directives represent regulations covering the amount of equity capital that insurance companies are required to hold in order to reduce the risk of insolvency. Depending on the categorization in the Solvency risk model, investments by insurance companies are required to be backed with more or less equity capital (European Commission, 2014).

8 The Dodd–Frank Wall Street Reform and Consumer Protection Act, signed in July 2010, is a major financial reform to promote the financial stability of the United States by improving accountability and transparency in the financial system. The Act established new government agencies and introduced several measures to increase stability and oversight (111th Congress of the United States of America, 2010).

9 The initial version of the Volcker Rule of the Dodd Frank Act prohibited banks to engage in proprietary trading and to invest in alternative asset classes such as hedge funds and private equity funds. In the final version, the ban to invest in hedge funds and private equity funds was abandoned whereas the ban on proprietary trading was implemented (111th Congress of the United States of America, 2010).

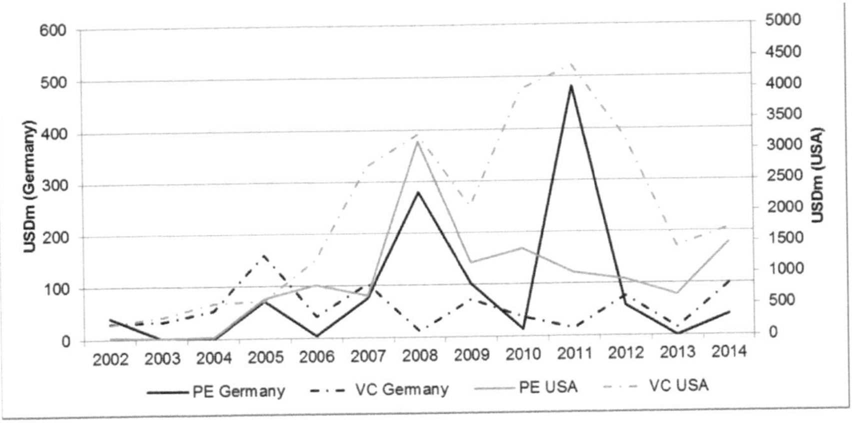

Figure 10 – New investment in CT (USA and GER) in USD bn

These numbers provide the background for our analyses of the perception of equity investors, policy makers and innovators to analyse potential influencing factors such as technology-immanent or regulatory factors or the financial crises and corresponding measures.

3.3.2 Data Collection

Based on our initial theoretical framework (see Figure 8) we approached suitable subjects. In addition to the entrepreneurs/innovators in CT firms active in different industry subsectors as well as the VC/PE investors and policy makers we added institutional investors to complement previous analyses. These investors act as limited partners for VC and PE funds but also invest directly or as co-investors. We applied a mixture of criterion sampling, purposeful sampling, and extreme sampling to schedule a first round of interviews in the United States and in Germany. For a second interview round, we shifted to snowball sampling, asking our interview subjects to identify key contacts who would be a valuable addition to our initial sample (Bewley, 2002).

We primarily gathered qualitative data gathered through semi-structured, open-ended interviews that lasted on average 55 minutes. These interviews collected perceptions of the CT 'finance-innovation-policy-nexus' by market participants. The interviews were led by researchers with significant industry experience who prepared the interviews through analyses of additional data, e.g. publicly available data and existing databases such as Bloomberg New Energy Finance (BNEF)[10] for specific investment deals and subsidy data and LexisNexis for newspaper articles and archival data on relevant policy measures. Through the use of multiple sources of data, we were able to support the depth of the interviews and gather suitable narratives to validate our interpretations (K. M. Eisenhardt, 1989).

We were interested mainly in subsectors in CT for which VC or PE financing was not intuitive (e.g., solar technology, advanced transportation, biomass), as it usually involves technology risks, what investors prefer to avoid (U. C. Haley & Schuler, 2011; Hargadon & Kenney, 2012; Schock, 2014). In addition, we strove to include extreme cases, i.e. CT firms that either were particularly successful or were not successful at all in securing PE capital. Moreover, our sample includes both PE firms that did and did not allocate capital to the CT sector.

At the point when the interviews did not yield significant new insights, we had reached an appropriate level of saturation and thus concluded the field work (Francis et al., 2010; Glaser & Strauss, 1967). We conducted a total of 64 interviews with executives in the CT sector, partners in VC firms, partners in later-stage PE firms, institutional investors, policy makers, and other stakeholders, 41 in the USA and 23 in Germany (see Table 6). A detailed list of interview participants can be found in the appendix (Table 16).

Region/ Interview partner category	United States	Germany
Cleantech companies	12	5
Venture capital	11	4
Private equity	5	6
Institutional investors	4	4
Policy makers/ executives	9	4
Total	41	23

Table 6 – Overview of Interviews in the United States and Germany

10 BNEF includes deal level data on investments and subsidies for most interviewed company, company investor or VC/PE investment firm.

3.3.3 Data analysis

For the purpose of structuring our analysis, we applied a theory-refinement approach (Creswell, 2003; Thomas, 2006). We went from very personalized accounts with rich information to accounts that were more aggregated, abstract, and analytical as well as embedded in our theoretical framework (Figure 8). This iterative process implied going back and forth between the raw interview data and the theoretical framework (Corbin & Strauss, 1994; Huberman & Miles, 2002). For instance after first interviews we concluded that the asset allocation by private institutional investors was key to a thriving environment of the VC/PE sector and, hence, institutional investors had to be included in our research, both theoretically and empirically. In our initial data analysis, we focused on the *perceptions of the interrelations* between the major actors along the 'finance-innovation-policy nexus' as our main *categories* for structuring and processing the incoming data. The established coding scheme is portraying the interrelations between the nexus of actors: Policy – Institutional Investors, Policy-VC/PE, Policy – Innovators, Institutional Investors – VC/PE, PE/VC – Innovators, Institutional Investors – Innovators (see Figure 11). The coding process resulted in 625 individual quotes. Based on these relationships we could explore the *direct* and *indirect* consequences of innovation policy and financial regulation.

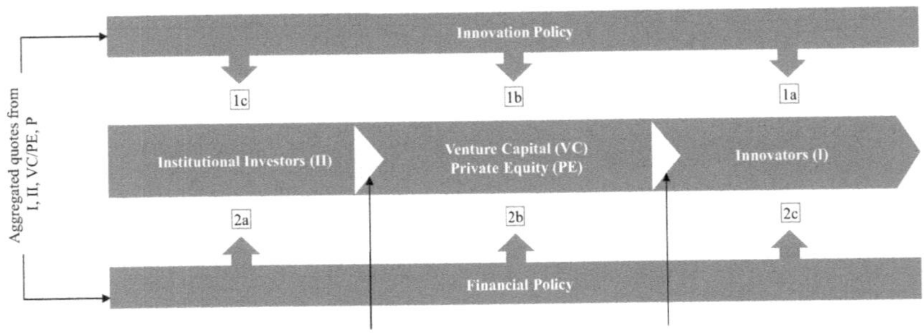

Figure 11 – Coding Process

We investigated the relationships among the primary actors of the 'finance-innovation-policy nexus', specifically emphasizing previously unstudied relationships with institutional investors and contrasting Germany and US. Within the actor driven coding scheme we looked for emerging themes during our open coding analysis (Glaser & Strauss, 1967); for instance, subsidy-dependence, (local) anchor investors or a mismatch of investment cycles or sizes emerged. The different quotes in the categories were aggregated into themes[11] by recognizing patterns in the data, that describe relationships between the various actors (see Figure 12). For example the role of anchor investors was mentioned by VC/PE funds and by limited partners alike, who both perceive the importance of an early and considerable involvement as key to a successful fundraising process. Thus we could verify the involvement of public investors as anchor investors in subsequent interviews.

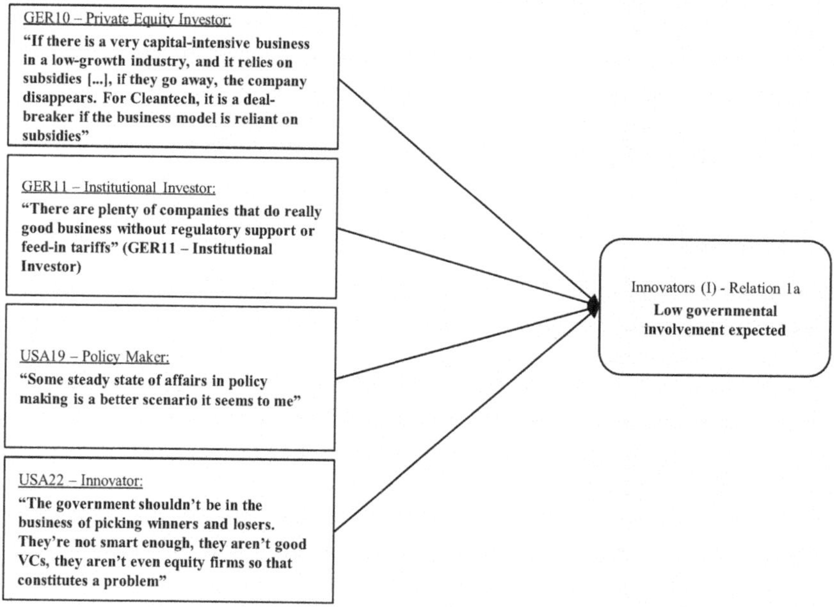

Figure 12 – Example of coding process

In our final step, we went beyond a mere presentation of patterns and descriptive comparisons to explain the reasoning behind the categories that were identified. Adopting a comparative case narrative we developed an understanding through organizing the different themes within, the 'finance-innovation-policy nexus' which has different characteristics in the US and Germany.

---

11 We refer to a theme when at least 3 interview participants coded in different relationships (categories) discussed a topic (Huberman & Miles, 2002; Patton, 2002).

To ensure the robustness of our analysis a number of measures have been taken (Moran-Ellis et al., 2006; Patton, 2002): Firstly, to ensure construct validity several data sources have been used (archival documents for the interview preparation, notes and interview transcripts). This allowed us to triangulate the understanding of a key concepts to avoid misinterpretation (Patton, 2002). Secondly, to ensure internal validity (avoiding alternative explanations) we compiled a multi-stakeholder sample (including policy makers and innovators) which includes typical cases across of a large set of technologies. This approach allows us to add to existing theory (Moran-Ellis et al., 2006). Thirdly, reliability was ensured by conducting the field research with two scholars, developing and refining the semi-structured interview guide for the interviews, recording and transcribing the evidence. Fourthly, we verified and extended the Anglo-German comparison by holding a workshop with scholars and practitioners active in the Cleantech sector.

3.4 Findings

Our main result is represented by the direct and indirect relationships in the 'finance-innovation-policy nexus' leading from institutional investors to PE and VC investors and ultimately to the innovators and which is accompanied by financial regulation and innovation policy. On the one hand, financial regulation targeting institutional investors causes trickle-down effects via PE and VC investors toward CT innovators (which are not *directly* affected by specific policy measures). On the other hand, we see effects of innovation policy on CT, VC/PE, and institutional investors. Examples of policy measures affecting the agents directly or indirectly are explained in the following findings sections. Summarizing tables (Table 7 and 8) for each of the relationships can be found at the end of sections 3.4.1 and 3.4.2 respectively. Tables 14 and 15 (in the appendix) provide additional individual quotes which support the following reasoning. Each of the quotes presented can be linked to the detailed interview descriptives by using the corresponding code (e.g. GER5).

3.4.1 Innovation policy (direct and indirect) effects

(1a) Innovation policy and Cleantech innovators

Policy makers put different mechanisms in place to either push technology or pull demand from the marketplace as a first-tier (direct) effect. In our discussions with market participants, we observed that technology push is mainly seen as suitable for R&D and seed phases. In comparison, later-stage technology push is regarded mostly as "picking winners." Consequently, in the US and Germany, investors and innovators alike prefer market-pull mechanisms like feed-in tariff or cash rebates at later stages, whereas straight tax incentives through rebates are seen as too dependent on the existence of taxable positive returns. From the perspective of VC investors direct influence or even investments by governmental authorities are not seen as helpful as they often distort the private sector: *"For Cleantech, it is a deal-breaker if the business model is reliant on subsidies"* (GER10 – PE Investor). Sometimes they compete with private market participants and affect their returns, or even crowd-out private investments. In early phases public officials stress the need for government involvement: *"The government is trying to make sure we grow the innovation base and provides a source of capital to get products out of the classroom to the market"* (USA6 – Policy maker).

Additionally, Germany-focused investors state that, government regulation can build up frameworks to strengthen innovative businesses. For innovators as well as VC investors, long-term and stable regulations are seen as the most important driver for adoption of technologies and investments in new and innovative companies. In particular, support through long-term and reliable measures fostering the demand side is regarded as an appropriate method to develop certain industries. The solar and wind industries are prime examples of CT industries that have flourished due to regulation provided by the German feed-in tariff. Policies with a similar mechanism are regarded favorably by innovators and investors alike. However, events such as the cancellation of feed-in tariff rules in Spain have given rise to a more skeptical view by investors and focus has shifted to business models entirely independent of support mechanisms, according to our interview partners from the investment world.

In the US, initiatives such as the Department of Energy Loan Guarantee Program (US-DOE LGP) are regarded as very important by some, but criticized by others. A former LGP official portrays it in the historical tradition of energy support mechanisms. *"The notion was that the government had an important role to play in the creation and the support of a new and important energy sector, much as the government has supported different kinds of energy development over the last hundred and fifty years*" (USA19 – Policy maker) (cf. Greentech Media, 2014). Investors see the program as problematic: "*The most unsuccessful program without question has been the loan guarantee program."* (USA11 – PE Investor). This ambivalence of the LGP was illustrated by stakeholders who discussed examples of firms that went bankrupt, resulting in loses for the taxpayer, most notably Solyndra or A123 on one hand, and cases that continue to be successful, such as Tesla on the other.

Compared to Germany, where regulation in the field of CT is perceived by all interview partners to be guided by stronger political will and social commitment towards sustainability, an existing but none the less fragmented und not coherent regulatory environment and support framework in the United States is observed: *"the subsidy environment and the understanding of the need for renewable energy is so much lower in the United States versus Germany"* (USA12 – Policy maker). Also PE investors state that: *"in the US there is really no regulatory inputs [on greenhouse gas emissions] at all for most of our companies"* (USA18 – PE Investor). This did not necessarily limit the adoption of renewable energy as can be witnessed through the additional capacity in wind and solar built in the US in recent years (IRENA, 2016).

Above all, market-driven adoption of technology through competitive prices and efficiency has been explained by investors and innovators alike to be a suitable way to achieve a sustainable transformation. VCs focus on business models independent of government support. Innovators and investors criticize that part of public money spent on "wrong" industries; however as businesses government initiatives could also fail as part of the innovation processes.

(1b) Innovation policy and private equity

In order to illustrate second-tier effects of innovation policy along the 'finance-innovation-policy nexus', we describe two policies that (indirectly) target PE albeit take effect at different levels. First, the U.S. LGP is particularly suitable for our discussion, because it represents an innovation policy that, apart from directly aiming at supporting CT innovators, is perceived to consider second-tier effects along the 'finance-innovation-policy nexus'. Despite the criticism of the "government picking winners" encountered by the program, the rationale for it is widely regarded as solid and well formulated. According to interview partners, the program was rightfully drawing on the expertise and resources of private investors to screen and select target companies. For instance, a former leading representative of the LGP stated, that *"the reason behind [the involvement of private investors] is that you want the private capital markets to tell you which projects they are supporting."* (USA19 – Policy maker) Thus, whereas the concept of the LGP considered second-tier effects, one reason for some of the more prominent bankruptcies of LGP recipients (Solyndra, A123) lies, according to investors, in the magnitude of the funds dedicated to the program and consequently to individual recipients. Although the executives managing the LGP were perceived by the interview partners with knowledge of the persons behind the program, to be highly skilled individuals, carefully investing more than $40 billion in less than two years is challenging, particularly if the investments are made in a sector characterized by market and technology uncertainties. Consequently, a major problem with the LGP according to PE investors was the fact that the individual funding round of at least $100 million was too large for some recipients. Hence some companies received too much capital too early in their corporate life cycle, which resulted in an aggressive growth strategy that made the companies vulnerable to adverse market changes as experienced in 2011.

Second, in contrast to the LGP, which had sufficient capital resources to further support companies that are already VC-backed, VC firms in Germany frequently are apprehended to struggle with scarce capital resources. Bearing in mind the success of the US VC ecosystem, many governments attempt to use VC as a tool of industrial policy, according to stakeholders in the field. Although private investors acknowledge this strategy, the implications of this policy can be serious. According to data by the European Private Equity & Venture Capital Association (EVCA) in 2011, around 40% of new funding for VC came from government agencies, compared to 10% in 2007 (Economist, 2012). Still, investors do not perceive public sources of capital alone as sufficient to create a sustainable investment environment. A VC investor asks for more: *"[A public initiative] gets to interact with the private sector in a really good way, so they do a lot of early stage funding for us and they create the opportunities for us to then invest in. It's indirect but very important."* (USA28 - VC) From the viewpoint of VC/PE and institutional investors, private local anchor investors are needed to trigger further international investments and to create a sustainable innovation environment. Most of the public programs, for example Germany's KfW-programs, aim at VC investments that have local, stage, and size-restrictions, which impose serious limitations on participating VC firms and often result in less than competitive returns as stated by parties involved. Return and risk determine the attractiveness of VCs in the eyes of institutional investors. Hence recent experience from institutional investors in the CT sector suggests that the returns of the field have not met expectations so far and consequently made fundraising more difficult for cleantech VCs, in particular compared to VCs investing in other industries. In Germany the role of public money in the investment field is perceived as highly important. As stated by investors and especially innovators in Germany, the lack of private institutional involvement at this stage leads to less money than demanded by innovators and insufficient fund sizes in general. Consequently this is seen to result in inadequate investment rounds for CT companies. Virtually all our interview partners, observed that Germany is struggling with a general lack of funds for PE, especially for CT. In other words, while US investors perceive public investment as potential competition, or even crowding-out, German investors view it as healthy and necessary complement.

(1c) Innovation policy and institutional investors

Finally measures that aim at innovators indirectly influence institutional investors as a 'third-tier' (indirect) effect. All interviewees acknowledge that governments are using large-scale investment programs or investment incentives to steer market participants. For instance, the emergence of the Cleantech VC industry is perceived to be closely connected to the Californian "Green Wave" initiative implemented by the pension funds California Public Employees' Retirement System (CalPERS) and California State Teachers Retirement System (CalSTRS). US investors often referred to the leading role of policy makers in mandating investments in certain asset classes or sectors such as CT with large volumes of dedicated funds, sometimes even overruling specific risk-return requirements. This regulatory push at a time when most of the underlying innovative companies in the CT field were at an early stage and did not need later-stage investment rounds created a boom period, which some see as a bubble, and led to unfulfilled expectations and poor returns at the fund level, as mentioned by public and private investors alike. Overspending at the initial phase of development led to an abrupt halt of investment. "The institutional investors engaged in the field are hesitant to pursue further investments until previous investments are returned and positive results are realized" (USA20 – Institutional Investor).

Similar to the US, institutional investors in Germany also contributed significant amounts of capital to the CT sector. The main difference from a regional point of view pertains to asset allocations that are used in the CT sector (see Figure 9): Unlike in the US, where institutional investors said to accept VC and PE in technology companies as an asset class, the preferred alternative of German institutional investors seem to be CT asset finance investments. In fact, the KfW (Kreditanstalt für Wiederaufbau) in Germany, a state-owned institutional investor continues to make significant investments in CT asset finance but ceased its capital commitments to German VC funds in 2012. "Real asset investing does not really have any upsides, but investors like it because its risks resemble fixed income investing." (GER11 – Institutional Investor)

Relationship / Geographical area	1a) Innovators (I)	1b) Private Equity (PE) /Venture Capital (VC)	1c) Institutional Investors (II)
Common	**Low governmental involvement expected** **Market-pull mechanisms preferred**	**Use of public money in CT sector ambivalent**	**Public money to leverage private funds necessary**
USA	**Changing support framework critical**	**Large fund sizes – private/public**	**Incentives to foster innovation needed**
GER	**Stable regulatory and institutional environment for sustainability beneficial**	**Lack of funds detrimental, but highly active public VC/PE sector**	**Support for assets/ infrastructure positive**

Table 7 – Perceptions of innovation policy for CT

3.4.2 Financial policy (direct and indirect) effects

(2a) Financial regulation and institutional investors

The second direction of interdependencies ranges from financial policy towards innovators. Institutional investors are driven by a balanced risk-return approach to increase their assets. Their work is subject to oversight by regulators and rating agencies, which play a role in limiting and selecting certain preferable asset classes. US and European investors reported on recent developments in the regulatory environment of the financial sector aimed in general at decreasing the appetite for risk. In the aftermath of the financial crisis, several regulations targeting the banking, insurance, and investment industries were introduced or tightened. Investors argued that *"there's a lot of quite unintelligent and uninformed drive to suppress risk particularly around the EU for all sorts of different agendas"* (GER11 – Venture Capital Investor). Thus the regulations influencing the financial industry at the institutional investor level—Basel III, Solvency II, the Dodd-Frank Act, and the Volcker rule —are seen as capable of limiting private equity fundraising. In the US, the regulatory changes anticipated by the Dodd-Frank act created the urge for institutional investors to divest riskier asset classes. In the CT sector, this led to a secondary market for institutional investor interests in CT funds, which were transferred to (institutional) investors with more risk taking capabilities at a discount. *"The threat of that [regulations to cover capital adequacy], I think, is quite profound so if a pension fund or an insurance company needs to reserve capital differently because it invests in a higher risk asset classes, you are clearly going to do less of it"* (GER11 – Venture Capital Investor). Some of the institutional investors, especially in Germany, would like to see more favorable regulation with regard to VC/PE. The possibility of diversification and higher return possibilities as well as the importance for economic development made them demand to allocate more private money in their pension plans or insurance assets in VC/PE.

In addition to the regulations, the uncertainty about anticipated regulatory changes impacts the investment behavior of institutional investors, according to investors from the US and Germany, resulting in fewer new investments in certain risky asset classes to anticipate limitations of risk. *"When you have economic and regulatory uncertainty people don't want to invest – you have a little bit of a lock up in the market"* (GER10 – Private Equity Investor). Decreasing allocations of VC by prominent institutional investors provide evidence for this development (Roth, 2012).

(2b) Financial regulation and private equity

Along the 'finance-innovation-policy nexus', policy measures directly targeted at institutional investors generate second-tier effects that influence the relationship between institutional investors and PE firms. The consequences of financial regulations implemented as a reaction to the financial crisis of 2008 at the second tier became apparent from the reaction of financial market participants interviewed. US investors argue that the undifferentiated approach in which risk is attributed to alternative asset classes within the regulatory framework does not adequately capture actual risk. According to VC/PE investors "a lot of government policy which has rightly been driving risk out of banking doesn't work out favorably in terms of the supply of venture capital" (GER15 – Venture Capital Investor).

Countries that exhibit a less developed institutional investor base, are perceived by investors to be affected more severely by a loss of anchor investors, which traditionally facilitated further fundraising for PE firms. According investors, the loss of state-owned banks in Germany, as limited partners for PE created significant challenges due to the lack of local pension funds and endowments that typically fund a large part of the total PE investments. In addition, large parts of institutional investor funds are concentrated in a relatively small number of increasingly large PE firms. Institutional investors stress their need for efficient capital allocation with less partners and therefore lower transaction costs. This is furthermore accelerated by the demand to allocate funds at the PE firms that fall in the top return quartile. A less diversified institutional investor base also creates challenges for smaller PE funds in attracting attention from fund investors. Traditionally, fund-of-funds have addressed this segment of the market but as an additional financial intermediary between institutional investors and PE funds, they are equally affected by the same regulatory frameworks. "[Fund-of-funds] add an extra fee layer [… / and] because they spread the money widely your returns will be fairly average" (GER15 – Venture Capital Investor). Particularly in the German market, investors see some unfavorable regulations, namely at the fund level, that impact the size of growth in capital markets. They often mention, the inability to transfer a loss carry-forward in case of a change in ownership hinders investments in R&D in young companies and hinders the typical VC investment model in Germany.

(2c) Financial regulation and Cleantech innovators

Although policy measures targeted at institutional investors at the first-tier level can increase or decrease PE funds at the second-tier, they ultimately increase or decrease capital availability for innovation at the third-tier level. Interview partners from all German actor groups feel capable to adapt to this situation, however, the impact can be more severe for certain segments of the real economy that are relatively more dependent on external sources of capital, especially asset-heavy sectors such as CT. VC investors with a track record of technology driven investments see themselves not capable to continue with their investment tradition. Our qualitative evidence indicates at least two areas that illustrate third-tier effects between PE and CT innovators: First, PE investors at the early and growth stages of the corporate life cycle frequently syndicate transactions in order to diversify their holdings and reduce portfolio risk. "Venture capital, more than any other asset class that we look at is a game of syndication, it's a game of participatory risk sharing. Anchor investors have a higher impact of catalyzing current investors and syndicate investors, into investments than a local venture capital fund" (GER13 – Institutional Investor). To stress the role of local capital a public investor told: "you can create all the policy framework you like in terms of trying to create a venture capital industry, but unless you're releasing local sources of capital for that, it will never succeed" (GER13 – Institutional Investor). According to PE investors, the larger a firm's capital requirements, the more important it is to find experienced co-investors to participate in the syndication. One argument frequently encountered in Germany during our interviews addressed the lack of PE firms with sufficient liquid funds to participate in such syndicated deals. Second, later-stage PE investors increasingly act as exit channels for VC investors. The lack of financial investors to provide an exit route can be severe if, at the same time, other exit routes, such as the public equity market or corporate mergers & acquisitions (M&A),

are not accessible. Since 2008, none of these options are perceived as economically viable by German investors.

Specifically, in the US CT sector, large capital requirements to scale asset-intensive businesses, coupled with the scarcity of syndication partners and long holding periods due to the lack of accessible exit channels, leads to rising skepticism toward future VC investment in the CT sector: "The Cleantech business does not easily match the business ecosystem of venture capital. It is capital intensive, it's highly illiquid and … the money is locked up for long periods of time" (USA 19 – Policy maker). Ultimately, the challenges associated with post-2008 Cleantech PE investments in general, and early-stage Cleantech VC investments in particular, culminate in the low return profile of many Cleantech dedicated funds. Still, an VC investor who regrets to not have invested in the automotive company Tesla Motors illustrates that challenges associated with the capital intensity of the capacity scale-up and the commercial feasibility can be managed by a combination of strong early- and growth-stage investors and accessible IPO markets, as well as, to some extent policy measures such as the loan guarantee program (LGP).

Relationship **Geographical area**	2a) Institutional Investors (II)	2b) Private Equity (PE) /Venture Capital (VC)	2c) Innovators (I)
Common	**Anticipated changes and regulatory uncertainty lead to "derisking" of asset allocations**	**Derisking of capital markets hit PE severely**	**Mismatch of CT characteristics and VC/PE**
USA	**Alternative asset classes with different characteristics get treated similar and therefore unfair**	**Money outflow limits new CT fundraisings**	**More mature growth capital and exit markets strengthen ecosystem**
GER	**Increasing regulatory obligations and overhead lead to market concentration**	**Unfavorable tax and reporting regulations restrict VC/PE**	**Narrow financial markets slow down development**

Table 8 – Perceptions of financial policy affecting CT

3.5 Discussion

The research question guiding our inquiry was: *How does the interplay between equity finance and corresponding policy measures influence (cleantech) innovation and entrepreneurship?* Below we reflect upon our results in the light of our theoretical background.

3.5.1 Financing innovation beyond VC/PE – the role of institutional investors

We find that there is a strong role for the financial sector beyond the innovator-VC relationship and the discussion of the fit of VC for cleantech investments, extending earlier work (Dimov et al., 2012; Hargadon & Kenney, 2012; Kenney, 2011a; Oakey, 2003; Petkova et al., 2014; Wonglimpiyarat, 2011). In times of market distortion, policy makers often decide to limit the fallout of capital imbalances. This merits an analysis of the interdependencies between the institutional environment, and the influence of financial policy and innovation policy in specific industrial sectors. Given the direct and indirect effects along a 'finance-innovation-policy nexus', an active role for financial policy has an impact beyond the direct targets of a specific policy (see Figure 13). The comparison of Germany and the US sheds light on these relationships. We therefore contribute to a more holistic understanding of equity markets for (cleantech) innovation and differentiate prior conceptual and empirical work (Kenney, 2011a; Kenney & Hargadon, 2012; Wonglimpiyarat, 2011).

On the one hand, the US loan guarantee program was designed to ease financial constraints on, for instance, clean technology firms and indeed did so very successfully. Nevertheless, in the case of the clean technology sector, the minimum capital drawdown was not in line with the technology life cycle. Consequently, some clean technology companies received far more capital than was required at their stage of the technology life cycle, thereby increasing the risks of being financially overextended and of later financial distress (relation 1b). However, this can also be seen as some form of government experimentation and an example of the entrepreneurial state (Mazzucato, 2013b). In addition innovation policy could target institutional investors to stimulate industry emergence e.g. by mandating investments in specific sectors; whereas in their absence these investments have to come from other sources (relation 1c).

On the other hand regulation thinned out European and more specifically German institutional investor base which led to difficulties in fundraising for VC/PE and thus capital constraints for the overall investment process in regard to syndication and follow on investments (relation 2b). Hence among the factors affecting innovation, institutional investors and their relationships with VC/PE play a significant role. Without their engagement a financing of industry emergence becomes very challenging (relation 2c).

The analysis reveals that the state (i.e. current investment flows between institutional investors and VC/PE) and structure (i.e. presence of local anchor investors) of underlying equity markets significantly shapes sector emergence and growth. With our analysis we extend recent work (Brossard et al., 2013a; Grilli & Murtinu, 2014; Revest & Sapio, 2013) by highlighting interdependencies between institutional investors and VC/PE companies that influence the finance environment for a specific industrial sector. Hence there is an additional way of supporting VC, namely targeted policy measures for institutional investors. This could alleviate the recent risk-averse behavior of VC/PE investors (Mazzucato, 2013a). In this regard we go beyond the fit of VC business models and cleantech innovation which faces a range of additional barriers. We also combine literature on the VC-policy relationship (in cleantech) with the more general literature on conditions for equity and VC markets (Bottazzi & Da Rin, 2002; Da Rin et al., 2006b; Lerner & Tåg, 2013a).

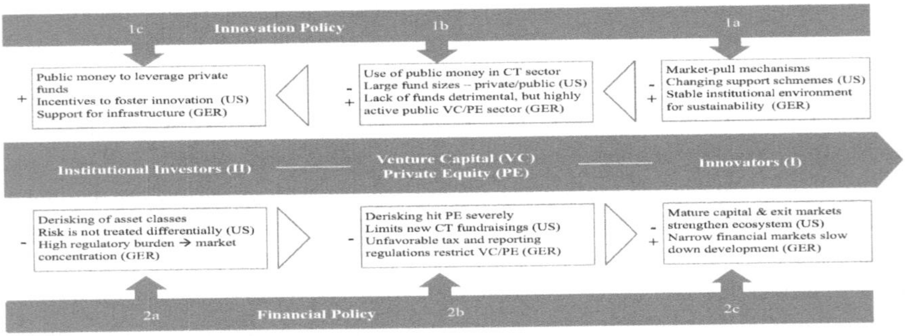

Figure 13 – Final model including relationships (based on findings)

3.5.2 Unintended policy consequences in financing industry emergence – the case of US and German cleantech markets

This paper investigates direct and indirect policy effects that affect actors not targeted by policy makers in the finance-innovation-policy relationship. First, we confirm prior research that market pull policies, especially feed-in tariffs (Mary Jean Bürer & Wüstenhagen, 2009; Criscuolo & Menon, 2015; Hoppmann et al., 2013) attract VC/PE investors into certain industries. This view is also shared by institutional investors, as critical actors supplying funds to VC/PE investors. Going beyond the R&D stage with subsidies or even equity investments, as highlighted by Olmos et al. (2012) is generally seen as critical throughout our study. Especially investors perceive the policy risk as high and they do not understand the behavior of public sector agents as co-investors. Regarding the general VC/Policy linkage we can confirm that, exit opportunities, favorable treatment of initial losses in the tax regime and capital market development (Bottazzi & Da Rin, 2002; Da Rin et al., 2006b; Lerner & Tåg, 2013a) are leverage points to stimulate VC/PE investments. In this regard institutional investors play a crucial role as they evaluate market opportunities before investing into new funds (relation 1b and 1c). We therefore confirm the notion that support schemes for VC in specific industries need to take into account the mechanisms in the equity markets to be effective (Lerner, 2002, 2009).

Second, conflicting aims of innovation and financial policy is the state of the financial industry in the aftermath of the financial crisis represent a case in point for indirect policy influences. Excessive risk taking and unbalanced risk-to-reward ratios were identified among the reasons leading to the financial crisis and recent corrective actions have been targeted at decreasing the risk exposure across all parts of the financial industry. While measures to decrease risk exposure can help to stabilize the state of the financial industry, the impacts of these measures usually lead to a drought of capital for innovators in small and medium-size enterprises (SME) (relation 2b and 2c in Figure 13). Policy makers need to differentiate between 'good and bad' risks as suggested by Mazzucato (2013a) in order to allow risky investments into VC/PE while at the same time limiting speculation in the financial markets.

There are key differences at the second tier between the United States and Germany with respect to the 2008 financial regulations. While the United States (still) exhibit an investor base with the potential to supply PE with substantial funds, there are comparatively fewer investors in Germany with PE experience (McCrone, 2015). The lack of local anchor investors is an obstacle to the fundraising process and can deter outside investors from committing capital, as capital markets are regionally dispersed (Destin, 2012). Therefore, PE faces some challenges in obtaining funding in the United States, and less resilient alternative investment markets in Germany might experience setbacks in their development, especially with respect to early-stage financing. VCs in the US and in Germany, especially in the clean technology and sustainability field, experienced difficulties in raising follow-on funds for their 2006-2008 fund generations (Knowles, 2013).

With our analysis, we add new perspectives on the linkages between financial policy and innovation policy (for an overview about policy blunders see Graham, 2005). Although the financial crisis is an exogenous shock, the systemic question of how financial policy is influencing the conditions for innovation, has been a relevant question for (national) policy. The comparison between Germany and US revealed that the institutional changes to reduce risk in asset allocations in the financial sector have affected the financing of US cleantech firms less than it affected German firms due to a robust and long-standing base of institutional investors.

Uncoordinated, individual policies, such as financial market regulation can have powerful ramifications for innovation outcomes that they do *not* target. In extension of previous literature on financing innovation (Mazzucato, 2013a, 2013b) and policy mixes (Flanagan et al., 2011b; Magro & Wilson, 2013) we underline the implicit role financial policy plays for innovation. Illustrated by the comparison between the United States and Germany, the economic (and environmental) policy stance regarding CT is quite different, while at the same time, the attitude toward financial policy is also different (Hess, 2014). Still, the coupling of objectives of long-term-oriented financial regulation with innovation policy incentives mitigates conflicts. Our empirical findings suggest that scholars should look for more trade-offs involved in decision making of policy makers by identifying other indirect effects (cf. Flanagan et al., 2011b).

3.6 Conclusions and policy implications

In this paper we studied the interdependencies between the financial sector and innovations in the clean technology sector, an industry highly influenced through regulation. We add institutional investors as important actors shaping the conditions for innovation by investing into VC/PE firms active in specific sub-sectors. Consequently, policy measures aiming at these institutional investors also affect innovation activities through an indirect effect from institutional investors over VC/PE firms towards innovating (small) companies. Investigating these hitherto understudied relationships between the financial system, namely institutional investors in the US and Germany, such as pension funds, and innovators and VCs as well as policy makers enabled us to identify unintended consequences at the intersection between financial sector and innovating firms. Hence policy makers are advised to look at this process from two perspectives: innovation policy and financial policy. The joint consideration allows them to differentiate their policy measures according to the state of the (institutional) investor market in corresponding regions. Anticipating indirect consequences through an advanced understanding of these mechanisms in the equity markets to mobilize private finance is warranted.

As every study, ours is not without shortcomings. Despite all efforts to secure theoretical saturation and holistic consideration in the qualitative data collection, we focused on perceptions of market actors rather than investment flows. Given the qualitative nature of this study, one limitation is based on the context-specific results. These include the sample of only two regions and a fraction of the CT universe. However keeping generalizability in mind during all steps of the research process, our sampling approach warrants a contribution for regulated environments and with comparatively high capital requirements such as nanotech or biotech. The comparative approach with the US and Germany in the CT field covers a broad range of the market, still other countries, especially China would be interesting to compare. We suggest further research on the complex interactions and interdependencies of the financial markets and policies complementing our qualitative analysis of perceptions with quantitative data and methods (i.e. investment flows) which could add to our understanding of interdependencies between financial and innovation policy, industry emergence and financial markets (cf. Schock, Mutl, Täube, & von Flotow, 2014).

Our research has implications for policy makers striving to effectively and efficiently foster (cleantech) industry emergence by private finance. We highlight possible conflicting objectives regarding underlying concepts such as the amount of risk taken by different actors involved in financing cleantech innovation. This requires a deep understanding of both the national characteristics and agents of the financial markets as well as their impact on firms operating in this (highly regulated) environment.

To put this statement into context, if the primary goal of policy makers is to stabilize the financial market by decreasing the risk exposure of its constituents, secondary economic-political targets are affected by this decision. In a recessionary environment, secondary targets could be vital to stimulating economic growth, accelerating innovation in certain industries or, in the case of Germany, manage the transition to an alternative energy system. Relating to these secondary goals, enterprises backed by PE firms have been found to generate relatively faster growth, while enterprises backed by VC firms have been found to be relatively more innovative than their peers. Despite these positive economic effects, both PE and VC, are deemed risky asset classes and therefore are directly impacted by policies targeted at institutional investors to limit risk in their portfolios.

In case governments view green growth as a priority, they need to address market and system failures, as well as consequences stemming from the interplay of financial and innovation policy. From our qualitative study, we can infer that isolated policy measures might not be conducive to green growth. In fact, our model shows that policy makers should try to anticipate consequences in equity markets and develop a clear and transparent strategy for the Cleantech sectors and sub-sectors which integrates financial institutions as distinct actors.

Given the different (national) institutional settings of the financial sector it is advisable to keep regulation adjusted to the characteristics and maturity of firms, industries, technologies and markets. Hence a general support of competition and new entry in order to mobilize the private finance for innovation and entrepreneurship (such as syndication, networking etc. (Lerner & Tåg, 2013a)) financial and innovation policy measures aimed at easing the early and growth stage private financing environment for clean technologies should be amended. For instance incentivizing market growth and stimulating competition or establishing new structures for public private cooperation, such as fund-of-fund concepts or public-private partnership funds aligned for national conditions (cf. Grilli & Murtinu, 2014).

3.7 Acknowledgements

The authors are grateful for the time and support of the interviewees. The paper benefited from feedback from Martin Kenney, John Zysman, Sanjay Jain, Brett Gilbert and other participants at the CFI-workshop at the Berkeley Roundtable on the International Economy (BRIE) in May 2012, the Babson College Entrepreneurship Research Conference (BCERC) 2012 in Fort Worth, TX, the RENT 2012 conference in Lyon, France, the DRUID conference 2013 in Barcelona, Spain and Marko Hekkert and other participants at the workshop on "Institutions and Entrepreneurial Development" in Utrecht, Netherlands, in November 2014 as well as from individual feedback from Paul Nightingale, Mariana Mazzucato and Carlota Perez during Friedemann Polzin's stay as visiting researcher at SPRU. All remaining errors are ours.

4 Public Policy Influence on Renewable Energy Investments – A panel Data Study across OECD Countries

Authors: Friedemann Polzin, Michael Migendt, Florian A. Täube & Paschen von Flotow

Abstract:

This paper examines the impact of public policy measures on renewable energy (RE) investments in electricity-generating capacity made by institutional investors. Using a novel combination of datasets and a longitudinal research design, we investigate the influence of different policy measures in a sample of OECD countries to suggest an effective policy mix which could tackle failures in the market for clean energy. The results call for technology-specific policies which take into account actual market conditions and technology maturity. To improve the conditions for institutional investments, advisable policy instruments include economic and fiscal incentives such as feed-in tariffs (FIT), especially for less mature technologies. Additionally, market-based instruments such as greenhouse gas (GHG) emission trading systems for mature technologies should be included. These policy measures directly impact the risk and return structure of RE projects. Supplementing these with regulatory measures such as codes and standards (e.g. RPS) and long-term strategic planning could further strengthen the context for RE investments.

4.1 Introduction

Climate change has been aggravating in recent years as CO_2 emissions continue to grow in developed and developing countries alike (IPCC, 2014). OECD countries have a larger responsibility to address climate change, as they accounted for almost 50% of the global carbon emissions in 2010, most of which were linked to the energy sector (BNEF, 2013; Müller, Brown, & Ölz, 2011; OECD, 2013a).

One possibility for transitioning towards a low-carbon society is to increase the share of energy (especially electrical energy) generated by renewable energy (RE) sources (Foxon & Pearson, 2007; Jefferson, 2008). To complement these activities, it is necessary to also increase overall efficiency of the energy sector (Eichhammer, Ragwitz, & Schlomann, 2013; Marques & Fuinhas, 2011; Schleich, 2009), however we focus on capacity additions of RE. Given limited financial resources of state governments, the involvement of private markets and investors is needed (Mathews,

Kidney, Mallon, & Hughes, 2010b). Investments in clean energy[12] companies, projects and infrastructure have been growing in the last decade and total up to a relevant amount. Yet the volumes are still relatively small when compared to investments in conventional fossil fuel-based power (see Figure 14) (BNEF, 2013).

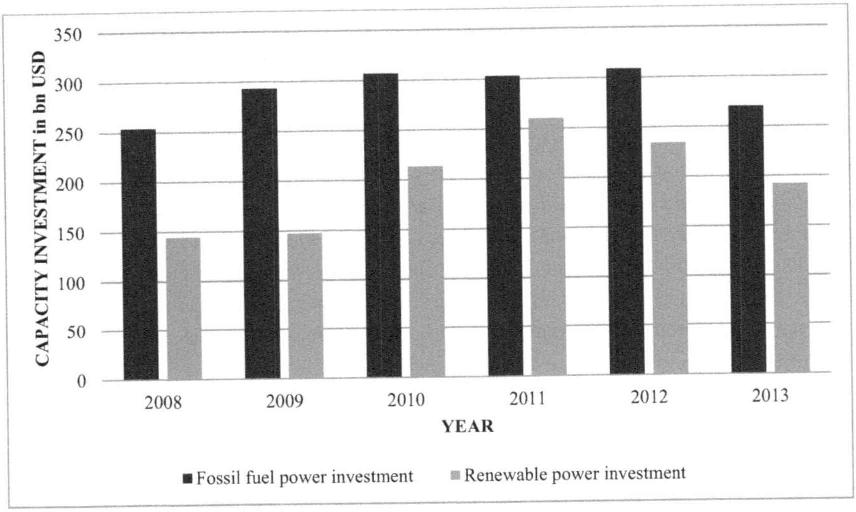

Figure 14 – Renewable power capacity investment compared to fossil-fuel power capacity investment, 2008-2013 in billion USD
(Adapted from Frankfurt School-UNEP Centre and BNEF (2014, p. 31)[13].

This is partially due to the challenge the diffusion of RE technology presents (Foxon & Pearson, 2007; Friebe, Flotow, & Täube, 2013; Friebe, von Flotow, & Täube, 2014; Veugelers, 2011). Market failures occur related to inherent characteristics of the energy sector (designed for fossil fuel-based power plants) on the one hand, as well as the particular nature of RE technologies on the other (Dinica, 2006; Helm, 2002; Jefferson, 2008; Wüstenhagen & Menichetti, 2012). Long payback periods and illiquid assets coupled with high regulatory dependencies and corresponding uncertainties often make RE unattractive or even unsuitable for investors. While this holds true for

12 Throughout this paper, we will use *renewable energy (RE)* and *clean energy* interchangeably.

13 Renewable energy does not include large hydro. Fossil fuel is gross investment in coal, gas and oil capacity and assumes retired fossil capacity is replaced. However a capacity retirement of 3.3% per year for coal, 4% per year for gas and 2.5% per year for oil is assumed. The numbers in this chart are adjusted for inflation.

mature technologies and conventional power plants, REs in addition face some technological uncertainty (Kenney & Hargadon, 2012; Mathews et al., 2010b).

To mitigate market failures and to compensate for technological and economic weaknesses, policy makers were historically confronted with a variety of options to stimulate diffusion of RE. This article attempts to uncover the effects of different policies to support clean energy applications. It adds to recent academic and political discussions about the choice among feed-in tariffs (FITs) and alternative mechanisms as well as the corresponding overall effectiveness and efficiency of these policy instruments (Carley, 2009; Lesser & Su, 2008; Mathews et al., 2010b). However quantitative analyses of the influence of public policies on investments in RE by private *institutional* investors are scarce (Bolkesjø, Eltvig, & Nygaard, 2014; Chassot et al., 2014; Lüthi & Prässler, 2011; Lüthi & Wüstenhagen, 2012b), with longitudinal, let alone panel data analyses almost non-existent. This is even more relevant since private institutional investors provide a significant amount of the funds deployed, particularly in certain more mature technologies such as wind (BNEF, 2013; IEA, 2013).

Thus, building on previous work on RE investor behavior (Bergek, Mignon, & Sundberg, 2013a; Chassot et al., 2014; Lüthi & Prässler, 2011; Wüstenhagen & Menichetti, 2012), we investigate the influence of public policies on subsequent RE investments by institutional investors across OECD countries over a time period of 12 years (2000-2011). Using a novel dataset gathered from Bloomberg New Energy Finance (BNEF) and the International Energy Agency (IEA) together with the International Renewable Energy Agency (IRENA), it applies a panel data regression. We develop policy implications adding to the academic literature of RE policies and RE investment decisions. The overarching research question is: Which policies have proven (most) conducive to investments in renewable energy assets?

The remainder of this paper is structured as follows: Section 4.2 briefly describes the conceptual motivation. Section 4.3 introduces the analytical method and data used. Section 4.4 presents the results and discussion while section 4.5 finalises with conclusion, limitations and next steps in the research process.

4.2 Theoretical background

4.2.1 Public policy influence on renewable energy deployment

Literature on energy policy has analysed the relationship between policy and RE deployment in a number of different ways, generating evidence for policy makers to support their decisions (Delmas & Montes-Sancho, 2011; Harmelink, Voogt, & Cremer, 2006; Jacobsson et al., 2009; Menz & Vachon, 2006). Fundamental questions such as influence of price or quantity-based mechanisms have been addressed (Menanteau, Finon, & Lamy, 2003). Prior research thus provides a differentiated picture to support RE deployment.

First of all, fiscal and financial incentives can be provided to accelerate the development of RE projects. A number of scholars (Bolkesjø et al., 2014; Couture & Gagnon, 2010; De Jager et al., 2011; del Río & Bleda, 2012; Jenner, Groba, & Indvik, 2013; Lesser & Su, 2008; Mitchell, Bauknecht, & Connor, 2006) underline the superiority of feed-in tariffs (FIT) to spur deployment and technological diversity and lower risks for private actors associated with RE technologies. These analyses hold when comparing FIT with other remuneration models such as quotas or auction-based systems (Butler & Neuhoff, 2008; Mitchell et al., 2006).

To provide short term fiscal relief for RE projects grants and subsidies can be provided to investors to reduce their overall cost for the projects (Bergek et al., 2013a; De Jager et al., 2011; Olmos et al., 2012). Similarly, government loans or loan guarantees could be of interest to private actors as the ability to refinance their activities is crucial for a long-term commitment in RE (Bergek et al., 2013a; De Jager et al., 2008, 2011). A growing stream of literature has further analysed the impact of tax-based incentives to spur RE deployment (Barradale, 2010; Bird et al., 2005; Cansino, Pablo-Romero, Román, & Yñiguez, 2010; Quirion, 2010). However, Barradale (2010) highlights the missing policy commitment (due to direct dependency on the public budget) as a main shortcoming of taxes and rebates.

Second, scholars argue that in the sense of carbon and energy market liberalisation preference should be given to market-based instruments as first best solutions, e.g. carbon cap and trading systems (Helm, 2002; Rogge & Hoffmann, 2010; Rogge, Schneider, & Hoffmann, 2011; S. Smith & Swierzbinski, 2007). Another market-based system, i.e. the tradability of RE certificates (green certificates) might further spur the deployment of renewables (Jensen & Skytte, 2002; Szabó & Jäger-Waldau, 2008).

Third, policy makers have the option to provide funds to local authorities to be spent on RE deployment (i.e. funds to subnational governments) (Bird et al., 2005; De Jager et al., 2008; Menz & Vachon, 2006; Ragwitz et al., 2008) or directly invest in complementary assets such as infrastructure (De Jager et al., 2008, 2011; Henriot, 2013; Steinbach, 2013).

In addition, investment decisions can be related to policy instruments that do not directly impact the risk and return structure of RE projects. For example, the perception of investment opportunities and preference for short term or long-term incentives also influence the decision to invest (Masini & Menichetti, 2012). Prior literature has found that the creation of the surrounding institutions is a major driver to facilitate investments in RE technologies (Bergek et al., 2013a; Wüstenhagen & Menichetti, 2012). This could be accompanied by a long-term strategic framework which is further valued by institutional investors as they prefer stability in cash flows over the duration of their investments (De Jager et al., 2008, 2011; Lüthi & Wüstenhagen, 2012b), thus foreseeable changes to regulations and policy consistency are paramount (W. White, Lunnan, Nybakk, & Kulisic, 2013).

Finally, regulatory measures to stimulate markets need to be established even though diffusion and application of RE technologies is socially and politically desirable (Jefferson, 2008). Furthermore, the highly regulated environment for diffusion of mature REs might require new forms of regulation compared to the commercialisation of RE in order to overcome market failures and dissolve path dependencies. Research has on the one hand highlighted mixed effects of renewable portfolio standards (RPS) for the US (Delmas & Montes-Sancho, 2011; Carley, 2009; Bird et al., 2005). Carley (2009), Bird et al. (2005), and Menz & Vachon (2006) show that RPS systems increase the share of RE produced but not the absolute amount, whereas Delmas and Montes-Sancho (2011) do not find a significant effect on RE capacity. On the other hand, further mandatory requirements, quota, and obligation schemes do exhibit a positive influence on RE application (Menz & Vachon, 2006), however, they have proven inferior to other instruments such as FIT (Butler & Neuhoff, 2008; De Jager et al., 2008, 2011; Mitchell et al., 2006).

One solution to address the problems encountered so far, apparently, is a ‘policy mix’ consisting of complementary instruments. However, no scholarly consensus exists on what the optimal policy mix could look like (Foxon & Pearson, 2007) or on which criteria should be applied to determine it (Carley, 2009). For example, Del Rio and Bleda (2012) argue that a variety of policies, consisting of technology-specific and technology-neutral measures is needed to enhance deployment of mature technologies. Relatedly, the question arises, if there is one optimal policy mix or several ones, contingent on different other factors?

Following this question scholars applied quantitative statistical methods (i.e. panel data analysis on country level) to investigate policy impacts on RE deployment. For example, Johnstone et al. (2010a) found that market based approaches favour technologies that are close to be technologically and cost wise competitive with fossil fuels (such as wind) whereas feed-in tariffs are conducive to innovation in less mature technologies (such as solar). On the other hand, Popp et al. (2011) do not find a significant effect of either FIT or a renewable certificate system on wind power investments.

Building on this work, scholars tried to uncover the influence of a number of different policy instruments on the contribution of renewables to the total energy supply (Marques & Fuinhas, 2012a). They show that aggregated measures such as fiscal and financial incentives (including FIT) as well as measures, that seek to define strategies and outline specific programs to promote these RE sources, have a positive significant impact. Controlling for a range of political (such as energy security and Kyoto protocol ratification) and socio-economic factors (e.g. prices for fossil-fuels, welfare etc.). Aguirre and Ibikunle (2014) found no significant positive influence of policies on RE growth, however they found a negative contribution of fiscal and financial incentives (i.e. taxes).

In sum, the literature has been searching for an integral overview of sustainable energy policy to spur RE diffusion. Given the mixed results of prior findings, we add to this debate through our research which aims at uncovering the effectiveness of different disaggregated policy instruments to induce private finance in RE assets. More specifically, we contribute to two different discussions: The FIT versus other support scheme debate, and the overall assessment of different support mechanisms for RE.

Beyond economic, regulatory and behavioural barriers, institutional factors such as acceptance among the local communities hinder the deployment of RE technologies (Arabatzis & Myronidis, 2011; Tampakis, Tsantopoulos, Arabatzis, & Rerras, 2013; Wüstenhagen, Wolsink, & Bürer, 2007). With our analysis we contribute to the private sector perspective on RE investments, leaving aside potential negative externalities caused by technologies deployed (Friebe et al., 2014).

4.2.2 Investors' perspective on renewable energies

The question of how to effectively mobilise financial resources for the deployment of RE and complementary infrastructure has been a major concern both in the academic and political debate (Bergek et al., 2013a; De Jager et al., 2011; Mathews et al., 2010b; Mowery, Nelson, & Martin, 2010b; Veugelers, 2011; Wüstenhagen & Menichetti, 2012). Mathews et al. (2010b, p. 3263) note that "the issue of public vs. private financing is not yet adequately explored", but add that there is consensus among policy makers that the transition to a low carbon economy will not happen without the involvement of private institutional investors (Müller et al., 2011; Popp et al., 2011).

Investments in RE deployment by institutional investors (i.e. investment/ pension funds, banks and insurance companies) are typically hindered by a number of factors; high upfront costs, risks, and uncertainty regarding long-term viability of the technology, long payback periods, high regulatory and infrastructural dependency as well as public acceptance (Cárdenas-Rodríguez et al., 2013; De Jager et al., 2011; U. C. V. Haley & Schuler, 2011; Kenney & Hargadon, 2012; Müller et al., 2011). These factors directly influence the risk/return profile of an RE investment, which is a major determinant for institutional investors (Cárdenas-Rodríguez et al., 2013; Dinica, 2006).

Bergek et al. (2013a) consider the evaluation criteria used by the heterogeneous group of RE investors, such as (overall or portfolio) cost, perceived (market) uncertainty and political risk. They argue that purely economic analyses (i.e. focusing on risk and return) fall short of capturing the wide range of factors influencing the decisions and processes for investing into RE technologies. Chassot et al. (2014) confirm this proposition by highlighting the moderating effect of worldviews, however, they highlight the perceived risk caused by policies as the main determinant of investment decisions. Based on insights from project developers, regulatory risks and the streamlining of the administrative process (grid access) have been identified as relevant decision criteria (Friebe et al., 2014; Lüthi & Prässler, 2011; Lüthi & Wüstenhagen, 2012b).

The ultimate requirement for a sustainable RE policy is a reduction of capital costs to create a level playing field with fossil fuel-based technologies which have been heavily subsidised in the past (Szabó & Jäger-Waldau, 2008). Thus, monitoring of these costs is crucial. Szabó & Jäger-Waldau (2008) suggest that a more competitive financial environment could actually reduce the costs of capital for RE projects, given that capital markets function efficiently. Therefore, a combination of supportive financial regulation and transparent policy making would be conducive to institutional investors to compete for building RE capacities (Bergek et al., 2013a; Lüthi & Wüstenhagen, 2012b; Wüstenhagen & Menichetti, 2012). This environment would in turn lower the perceived regulatory risk and, thus, lower the financing costs for RE projects while still allowing reasonable rates of return. Decreasing support corresponding to technological development, meaning adaptive policy making, can furthermore spur the deployment of more innovative technologies (Szabó & Jäger-Waldau, 2008).

With our analysis we explore which policy instruments have been conducive to RE investments by institutional investors, thus we examine this relationship over time. We answer the call for research of Wüstenhagen & Menichetti (2012) by specifically investigating the role of policy on the perception of institutional investors.

4.3 Methods and data

4.3.1 Research design

Investigating the diffusion of a particular technology and corresponding investments requires a longitudinal research design (Angrist & Pischke, 2008; Cárdenas-Rodríguez et al., 2013; Johnstone et al., 2010a; Popp et al., 2011; Wooldridge, Calhoun, Jung, Greber, & Montgomery, 2009). Prior literature applied panel data regressions at the EU level (Bolkesjø et al., 2014; Marques & Fuinhas, 2012a) with a few comparing OECD or BRIC countries (Aguirre & Ibikunle, 2014; Cárdenas-Rodríguez et al., 2013; Johnstone et al., 2010a; Popp et al., 2011).

Building on these methodological approaches we cover a variety of OECD countries, conducting a panel data regression throughout the time period from 2000 to 2011 to explain the influence of policy instruments on the diffusion of clean energy technologies. As policy instruments do not exhibit an immediate effect on technology application and investments, we add a lag procedure which is explained in section 4.3.3.4 (Wooldridge et al., 2009). The time frame is chosen due to the limited availability of high quality data, and as it still covers the most substantial developments in the worldwide renewable energy sector, especially regarding the involvement of institutional investors.[14] Globally the wind sector grew from 18 GW installed capacity in 2000 to 238 GW installed capacity in 2011, while the solar sector grew from 1.5 GW installed capacity in 2000 to 67 GW installed capacity in 2011. The biomass sector, at the same time, grew from 38 GW installed capacity in 2000 to 74 GW installed capacity in 2011 (IEA, 2014).

4.3.2 Data

Data was collected from two independent data sources. Investments (additions in RE capacity) have been drawn from BNEF, which possesses one of the most comprehensive databases in the field of clean technology financing (Cárdenas-Rodríguez et al., 2013). It contains information on installed electricity generating capacity, date, transaction type, financing type, amount of equity, and amount of debt. We used data from 2003 to 2011. The complete database includes 5840 Solar

14 When using data from BNEF, one has to be aware of the fact that the data is being updated after a certain year. Thus we have chosen to limit the data of the dependent variable to 2011, as this timeframe covers the most reliable data quality.

Investments, 9643 Wind Investments and 2889 Biomass & Waste Investments. These three RE subsectors account for 72% of the RE funds invested and with 74 GW installed for 75% of all capacity additions in the period, and have therefore been selected for further analysis. The records of the BNEF database start with the year 2003 and we further decided to use the data up to the year 2011, as data quality of the following year did not meet the standards of previous years at the time of research in early 2013.

Policy indicators were drawn from the IEA/IRENA Policy and Measures (PM) database which includes policy measures in OECD countries from 1974 onwards. These indicators have been used by scholars to analyse the impacts of aggregated policy instruments in Europe (Cárdenas-Rodríguez et al., 2013; Marques & Fuinhas, 2012a, 2012b) and globally (Aguirre & Ibikunle, 2014). We used the IEA/IRENA policy measures data from 2000-2011 which corresponds to the availability of investment data. The database includes a total of 957 distinct policy measures active in the respective years resulting in 7835 policy data points (see appendix Table 18).

We structured the data according to sectors (Multiple RE sources, Wind, Solar, and Biomass) and applied additional data processing: First, we removed cases with missing values and included only completed deals. Second, our interest in the influence of policy measures lead to the exclusion of countries with less than three consecutive years of investor activities (DV). The case-selection is carried out for each sector analysed (see section 4.3.3. for the procedure and Table 17 (in the appendix) for a list of countries in the subsamples). The selection of policy instruments included in the model is described in section 4.3.3.2.

As control variables we further included macroeconomic and energy market data from the US Energy Administration - EIA (carbon intensity of the economy), OECD (Long-term interest rates, share prices) and from the World Bank (Total energy consumption, gross domestic product (GDP)) in our analysis.

4.3.3 Model

We investigate the influence of the set of different policy measures on subsequent investments into RE capacity by institutional investors. The components of this model are shown in Figure 15.

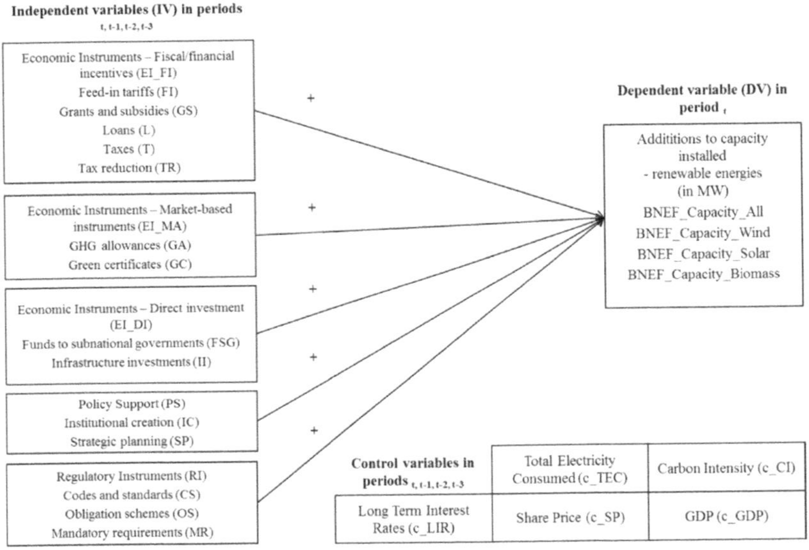

Figure 15 – Model for the quantitative panel regression

The five different subsets of policies include 957 different (countries and time series generated) measures of which some are active in every sector, while some are active in a single sector only. The included variables are log-transformed to correct for the skewed distribution of both dependent and independent variables (Hair, 2010). We expect to see a positive influence for every subset of policies on the capacity additions (see Figure 15).

4.3.3.1 Dependent variable (DV)

The dependent variable, drawn from BNEF, for the overall model is measured as aggregated newly installed capacity (in MW) in a certain country and year in a specific subsector (e.g. solar, wind, biomass). We use capacity indicators as they are seen as the most accurate proxy for the deployment of a technology (Popp et al., 2011).

4.3.3.2 Independent variables (IV)

The main independent variables were drawn from the IEA/IRENA database. We constructed our indicators by counting distinct policies per country per year (see Table 18 for a complete categorisation). They are measured by the number of active instances of policies affecting the RE sector (Johnstone et al., 2010a; Marques & Fuinhas, 2012a). We call these counts 'accumulated number of RE policies and measures' (ANPM) (Aguirre & Ibikunle, 2014). The active policy instances are used as an ordinal variable with the assumption that the more policies (of a kind) the better for investments. This allows comparing the experience of many countries and decomposing the effect of distinct factors econometrically (Cárdenas-Rodríguez et al., 2013).

We can further distinguish between technology specific instruments (e.g. specific targets for certain energy sources) and instruments that apply to all types of RE (e.g. German FIT). The IEA/IRENA PM database provides relevant information on characteristics (title, country, year (started and ended), policy status (e.g. in force, ended, superseded), policy type, policy target (e.g. subsector such as solar, wind and biomass), geographical scope (supranational, national, regional), policy sector (e.g. electricity, multi-sectoral, framework policy), size of plant targeted (large, small or both) and funding (partially, depending on instrument)). We build our model with distinct policies as independent variables based on prior literature reviewed in section 4.2.

4.3.3.3 Controls

To account for technological progress, economies of scale as well as the fact that the installed capacity gains momentum (leading to variance from the previous years), we include year and country dummy variables. To rule out alternative explanation for RE investments we included a number of control variables in the regressions. Economies of scale are picked up by the time dummy variable and therefore not included among the control variables. Further economic indicators that might drive capacity additions include the GDP (c_GDP). To account for differences in energy use and consumption we include energy dependency (CO_2 intensity – Metric Tons of Carbon Dioxide per thousand year 2005 U.S. dollars GDP) as well as electricity consumption in the regression (c_CI, c_TEC). Finally, to account for factors influencing investor behaviour, we include interest rates (c_LIR) as well as share prices (c_SP) of local indices as these might render an investment into RE vs. non-RE more or less attractive.

4.3.3.4 Lag structure

As common for longitudinal analyses we assume that the independent variable affects the dependent variable immediately and with a certain delay. This relation is included in our model through a lag structure where we compare the respective time values of the DV with several different time values of the IV. This approach helps in this case to account for the time-dependent influence of policy measures on investor behaviour (Angrist & Pischke, 2008; Wooldridge et al., 2009). We decided to introduce a lag structure with a lag of the policy effectiveness within zero to three years (i.e. investments in capacity in year $_{t}$ are influenced by policy measures in years $_{t,t-1,t-2,t-3}$). This means policies could have a direct effect on investor decisions or it could take up to three years for a policy to trigger a capacity addition. On the one hand, it is possible that investors anticipate the regulation and already have their projects ready when it is passed, as the regulatory process is mostly open. On the other hand, there are factors delaying the investment process such as the time needed to build the wind farm or solar park and to gain access to the grid. In general, changes in regulations evolve throughout time and are communicated prior to them being passed and set active.

4.3.4 Longitudinal analysis (panel data regression)

Prior research acknowledges that determining the influence of policy measures on investments in RE capacity is challenging since spatial and temporal effects could overlap (Marques & Fuinhas, 2012a; Marques, Fuinhas, & Pires Manso, 2010). Following their work we assume panel auto-correlation and contemporaneous correlations as similarities in policy design (e.g. in EU countries) and a tendency to increase the number of policy measures which can be observed throughout the data. The literature reviewed in section 4.2 analyses policy measures that are conducive to RE investments, which are included in the model (see section 4.3.3.2). The best fitting econometric technique is to use a panel data approach under the conditions resulting from characteristics of policy making (Marques & Fuinhas, 2012a).

We estimate panel corrected standard error (PCSE), ordinary least squares (OLS) and random effects estimator (REE) models. Following Marques and Fuinhas (2012a) and to mitigate errors resulting from the data structure, we use several econometric treatments: Heteroskedasticity, panel autocorrelation, and contemporaneous correlation are addressed through fitting approaches (Reed & Ye, 2011). Thus, we circumvent inefficient coefficient estimation and a biased estimation of standard errors (Marques & Fuinhas, 2012a). We do not focus on OLS or REE as they do not address serial correlation and contemporaneous correlation, however, we include the estimates for reasons of robustness (Marques & Fuinhas, 2012a, 2012b).

Our analysis proceeds as suggested by Marques and Fuinhas (2012a) : 1. We observe the quality and nature of the data; 2. We test the presence of heteroskedasticity, panel autocorrelation and contemporaneous correlation; 3. If the results do not conform to standard assumptions about errors (i.e. if the error terms are Independent and identically distributed – iid), we employ the PCSE estimator, which is a suitable solution to improve the accuracy of the estimators; 4. We compare the results with those derived from OLS and REE to check the robustness.

	Random effects / Pooled OLS				Fixed effects			
	Multiple RE	Solar	Wind	Biomass	Multiple RE	Solar	Wind	Biomass
Modified Wald test	-	-	-	-	236.84 ***	91.24 ***	1052.72 ***	141.05 ***
Wooldridge test F(N(0,1))	19.20 *** (OLS)	12.63 *** (OLS)	19.62 *** (OLS)	1.22 (OLS)	-	-	-	-
Pesaran's test	19.55 ***	5.54 ***	16.26 ***	8.70 ***	15.02 ***	4.13 ***	10.15 ***	4.61 ***
Frees' test	3.00***	1.03***	2.49***	0.90***	2.34***	0.22	1.87***	0.63**
Friedman's test	78.00***	30.63***	63.77***	38.51***	25.35**		45.38**	27.18*

Notes: The Wald test has a Chi2 distribution and tests the null hypothesis that none of the independent variables are significant; The Wooldridge test is N(0,1) distributed and tests the null hypothesis that there is no serial correlation. Pesaran and Frees' tests examine the null hypothesis that there is cross-sectional independence; Pesaran's test is a parametric procedure which follows a standard normal distribution; Frees' test employs Frees' Q-distribution; Friedman's test is a non-parametric estimation based on Spearman's rank correlation coefficient (Aguirre and Ibikunle, 2014; Hoyos and Sarafidis, 2006; Marques and Fuinhas, 2012a). ***, **, *, denote 1, 5 and 10% significance level, respectively. xtcsd and xtserial commands were used.

Table 9 – Specification tests for the quantitative model

Table 9 presents results from the estimations of the specification tests regarding quality and nature of the data and confirms that especially the policy data is heteroskedastic (i.e. has a common variance) and that panel autocorrelation and contemporaneous correlation is present. Hence we use PCSE estimator as main econometric analysis technique.

As public policy effects differ across RE subsectors (e.g. solar, wind, biomass) we carried out the further analysis sector by sector and also aggregated the data (Multiple

RE sources) to analyse effects that are similar across sectors. Thereby, we can also distinguish policy instruments between the sectors as well as policies that apply to all sectors.

Panel data estimation without lag procedure (I)

$$\mathrm{IC}_{jk} = const + \sum_{i=1}^{i} \beta_i PM_{ijk} + C_{jk} + d_j + d_k + \varepsilon_{jk}$$

Panel data estimation with lag procedure (II-IV)

$$\mathrm{IC}_{jk} = const + \sum_{i=1}^{i} \beta_i PM_{ijk-l} + C_{jk-l} + d_j + d_k + \varepsilon_{jk-l}$$

IC_{jk} is the aggregated installed capacity financed by institutional investors per country j per year k. PM_{ijk} is a vector of i explanatory variables representing policy measures based on the IEA/IRENA scheme (per country per year). C_{jk} consists of a number of control variables (Model I). For the analyses of time-dependent phenomenon we include lags l of one to three years in the regressions (Model II-IV). The dummy variables d_j and d_k refer to country and time, respectively. The PCSE estimator permits the error term ε_{jk} to be correlated over the cases (i.e. countries). Moreover a first-order autoregression for ε_{jk} over time can be used. Finally the estirmator allows ε_{jk} to be heteroskedastic (Cameron & Trivedi, 2009; Marques & Fuinhas, 2012a).

4.4 Results and discussion

The aim of our research is to uncover the influence of different policy instruments on subsequent investments in RE by private institutional investors over time in a longitudinal research design. Policy makers interested in improving their country's transition towards RE should implement measures for attracting private institutional investors, as the capital required for large-scale RE projects by far surpasses the available funds of utility companies as well as the public budgets. Institutional investors' capital played an important role in the development of the RE sector, and establishing a favourable environment for them, including specific policies, should increase capacity additions in the future. With our analysis we provide an integral picture of RE policies and their influence on RE capacity investments by institutional investors. We intend to contribute to the literature surrounding investor behaviour regarding RE technologies, as investors provide funds for large scale deployment (Bergek et al., 2013a; Lüthi & Prässler, 2011; Wüstenhagen & Menichetti, 2012).

The analysis is conducted on a sectoral basis to allow differentiated policy recommendations. In the following discussion, we highlight significant effective and ineffective policy measures and relate our results to previous studies in this literature stream (Aguirre & Ibikunle, 2014; Marques & Fuinhas, 2012a; Marques et al., 2010).

Table 19 (in the appendix) shows the descriptive statistics of our analysis. The correlation among explanatory variables has been subject to analysis as well. The simultaneous use of several drivers leads to the hypothesis of collinearity among explanatory variables. Table 19 and Table 20 (in the appendix) show the summary statistics and the correlation coefficients for our analysis. The analysis suggests the absence of collinearity among the exogenous (independent) variables.

Independent variables (ANPM) (t-1)	PCSE							
	No autocorrelation		No autocorrelation		No autocorrelation		No autocorrelation	
	Multiple RE		Wind		Solar		Biomass	
	(I)		(II)		(III)		(IV)	
	Coeff.	S.E.	Coeff.	S.E.	Coeff.	S.E.	Coeff.	S.E.
EI_FI_FI$_{ijk}$	0.69***	0.28	0.70***	0.26	1.18***	0.26	0.09	0.24
EI_FI_GS$_{ijk}$	0.33	0.25	0.13	0.24	0.61***	0.23	0.61**	0.24
EI_FI_L$_{ijk}$	-0.36	0.26	0.30	0.27	-0.91***	0.30	-0.16	0.32
EI_FI_TR$_{ijk}$	0.40**	0.18	0.20	0.20	-0.01	0.28	0.10	0.18
EI_FI_T$_{ijk}$	-0.90*	0.48	-0.51	0.34	1.00**	0.45	-0.20	0.29
EI_MI_GA$_{ijk}$	1.48**	0.62	1.59***	0.41	-1.17**	0.60	0.97*	0.47
EI_MI_GC$_{ijk}$	-0.02	0.34	-0.03	0.35	-2.27***	0.41	0.06	0.34
EI_DI_FSG$_{ijk}$	-0.65*	0.40	-0.38	0.43	-1.43***	0.45	1.50***	0.39
EI_DI_II$_{ijk}$	0.15	0.26	0.37	0.24	0.21	0.40	-1.20**	0.39
PS_IC$_{ijk}$	-0.41	0.28	0.13	0.26	-1.51***	0.38	0.83**	0.37
PS_SP$_{ijk}$	0.70*	0.37	0.16	0.43	2.35***	0.30	-0.44*	0.24
RI_CS$_{ijk}$	0.45***	0.17	0.63**	0.19	0.54**	0.27	-0.41	0.37
RI_OS$_{ijk}$	0.28	0.26	-0.09	0.31	0.16	0.31	-0.01	0.27
RI_MR$_{ijk}$	0.52	0.36	0.21	0.32	0.77**	0.37	0.28	0.27
Control variables								
c_TEC$_{ijk}$	0.64	0.22	0.75**	0.36	0.95	0.74	-1.97***	0.65
c_CI$_{ijk}$	-0.09	0.67	1.94**	0.94	-6.01***	2.24	4.37***	1.56
c_LIR$_{ijk}$	-0.67***	0.19	-0.66***	0.19	-0.54	0.75	-0.57**	0.29
c_SP$_{ijk}$	1.84***	0.56	1.58***	0.62	-0.24	0.59	0.61	0.42
c_GDP$_{ijk}$	-0.02	0.08	-0.06	0.08	-0.82	0.70	2.16***	0.58
_cons	-7.12**	3.29	-6.74**	3.47	21.59	17.18	-53.24***	13.25
Observations	330		319		176		220	
R2	0.38		0.40		0.49		0.38	
Wald	258.81***		208.87***		161.69***		169.40***	

Notes: The Wald test has a Chi^2 distribution and tests the null hypothesis of non-significance of all coefficients of independent variables; panel corrected standard errors are reported. ***, **, *, denote significance at 1, 5 and 10% significance levels, respectively; Estimates include country and time dummies (Marques and Fuinhas, 2012a). xtpcse command was used.

Table 10 – Panel-corrected Standard Errors (PCSE) Regression Results

We estimated all models separately using the PCSE and the OLS estimator as well as REE for robustness checks. We conducted the analysis for Multiple RE data and distinct sectors. The estimation results are displayed in order of the categories and different policy structures. We report the results with models based on a time lag of 1 year, thus, investments lagging behind the introduction of policy by 1 period. With this analysis we go beyond extant work (Aguirre & Ibikunle, 2014; Johnstone et al., 2010a; Marques & Fuinhas, 2012a), ruling out reverse causality (i.e. investments driving policies for example through lobbying) and providing a more realistic approach to renewable deployment, taking into account a lagging reaction of investors to policy measures. The results of our complete policy variable analysis are presented in Table 10 and in Table 11. An overview about our results can be drawn from Table 12.

Independent variables (ANPM) (t-1)	OLS							
	Standard errors Multiple RE (V)		Standard errors Wind (VI)		Standard errors Solar (VII)		Standard errors Biomass (VIII)	
	Coeff.	S.E.	Coeff.	S.E.	Coeff.	S.E.	Coeff.	S.E.
$EI\_FI\_FI_{ijk}$	0.69**	0.30	0.70***	0.26	1.18***	0.31	0.09	0.26
$EI\_FI\_GS_{ijk}$	0.33	0.26	0.13	0.25	0.61**	0.25	0.61**	0.25
$EI\_FI\_L_{ijk}$	-0.36	0.44	0.30	0.40	-0.91**	0.43	-0.15	0.39
$EI\_FI\_TR_{ijk}$	0.40	0.33	0.20	0.29	-0.01	0.34	0.10	0.27
$EI\_FI\_T_{ijk}$	-0.90*	0.49	-0.51	0.44	1.00*	0.58	-0.20	0.39
$EI\_MI\_GA_{ijk}$	1.48**	0.67	1.59***	0.61	-1.17	0.80	0.97	0.53
$EI\_MI\_GC_{ijk}$	-0.02	0.44	-0.03	0.41	-2.27***	0.48	0.06	0.37
$EI\_DI\_FSG_{ijk}$	-0.65	0.52	-0.38	0.47	-1.43***	0.47	1.51***	0.52
$EI\_DI\_II_{ijk}$	0.15	0.44	0.37	0.37	0.21	0.56	-1.20***	0.46
PS_IC_{ijk}	-0.41	0.41	0.13	0.34	-1.51	0.43	0.83**	0.36
PS_SP_{ijk}	0.70**	0.35	0.16	0.36	2.35***	0.34	-0.44	0.30
RI_CS_{ijk}	0.45	0.33	0.63**	0.32	0.54	0.36	-0.41	0.33
RI_OS_{ijk}	0.28	0.39	-0.09	0.35	0.16	0.41	-0.01	0.34
RI_MR_{ijk}	0.52	0.37	0.21	0.34	0.77*	0.47	0.28	0.31
Control variables								
c_TEC_{ijk}	0.64***	0.19	0.77***	0.20	0.95	0.72	-1.97***	0.52
c_CI_{ijk}	-0.09	0.96	0.96	1.02	-6.01**	2.58	4.37***	1.60
c_LIR_{ijk}	-0.67***	0.24	-0.74***	0.24	-0.54	0.67	-0.57*	0.30
c_SP_{ijk}	1.84***	0.33	2.10***	0.35	-0.24	0.46	0.61*	0.37
c_GDP_{ijk}	-0.02	0.10	-0.05	0.09	-0.82	0.70	2.16***	0.50
_cons	-7.12***	2.65	-8.33***	2.59	21.59	17.01	-53.24***	11.51
Observations	330		319		176		220	
R2	0.38		0.40		0.49		0.38	
F	10.05***		10.93***		8.01***		6.52***	
Mean VIF	2.03		1.94		9.17		5.15	

Notes: The F-test is normally distributed N(0,1) and tests the null hypothesis of non-significance of the coefficient estimates taken together. ***, **, *, denote significance at 1, 5 and 10% significance levels, Estimations include both country and time dummies (Marques et al., 2010). regress command was used.

Table 11 – Ordinary Least Square (OLS) Regression Results

4.4.1 Fiscal and financial incentives

First of all, our results highlight the effectiveness of FIT to spur capacity additions which directly impact the risk and return structure of RE projects as a policy instrument that guarantees a certain return on investment and provides an incentive for investors. FIT have been implemented in a range of countries, starting with Germany and Austria in 2000. The aggregated results (Multiple RE) as well as wind and solar sector results revealed a highly significant positive coefficient. However, the effect differs across sectors. Whereas in the solar sector FIT has a stronger impact than overall, FIT is less effective in the wind sector.

FITs proved particularly successful in countries such as Germany and Italy with some exceptions in other countries (e.g. Spain) (Bolkesjø et al., 2014; Couture & Gagnon, 2010; del Río & Bleda, 2012; Jenner et al., 2013; Lesser & Su, 2008; Mitchell et al., 2006). This instrument is a strong signal to investors as it addresses the capital market restrictions by adjusting the risk/return structure (Cárdenas-Rodríguez et al., 2013). Thus our research is in line with evidence by Río and Bleda (2012) who underline the superiority of FITs to spur deployment and to lower risks associated with RE technologies. In addition our research confirms that a variety of policies consisting of specific and technology-neutral measures spur RE technology deployment.

Second, our results show that grants and subsidies prove to be effective as short term measures to alleviate finance constraints. This holds true for the solar and biomass sectors. Grants and subsidies temporally reduce the cost of finance for a project, and directly depend on a public budget (Johnstone et al., 2010a) which makes them more unstable than for example FIT. This is shown by our results of the solar sector. Institutional investors exhibit a preference of FIT over subsidies. With this analysis we confirm earlier work, that highlighted this type of support instrument can also contribute during the diffusion stages of the innovation cycle (Bergek et al., 2013a; Bolkesjø et al., 2014; Olmos et al., 2012).

Third, we provide evidence for the effectiveness of loans and loan guarantee programs. According to our results this type of instrument does not spur the deployment in the solar sector. This stands in contrast to prior literature which showed that loans and loan guarantees could enhance institutional investors ability to refinance by reducing cost of capital (Bergek et al., 2013a; De Jager et al., 2008, 2011)

Our research regarding tax-based measures revealed mixed evidence. On the one hand aggregated results point towards a negative effect of taxes on subsequent capacity additions in renewables; however results from the solar sector reveal a positive impact. On the other hand, tax reductions tend to increase overall capacity in renewables, with no particular effect in the sectors. We therefore confirm earlier research that pointed towards an ambivalent nature of taxes as they depend on public budgets (Barradale, 2010; Cansino et al., 2010; Quirion, 2010).

Above all we confirm (Marques & Fuinhas, 2012a) who found that fiscal and financial incentives are conducive to increasing the share of RE. We extend their results by decomposing the indicator into distinct policy measures. On the other hand, we contrast and extend Aguirre and Ibikunle (2014) who found a negative effect of fiscal and financial incentives. We disentangle this view, showing that FIT and grants and subsidies can have positive effects; however, we do find a negative effect for taxes.

Institutional investors' decisions are supported through direct influence on their return side of their investment calculations. Higher income through grants and subsidies and lower capital costs through FITs support their openness towards RE investments (Lüthi & Wüstenhagen, 2012b). Tax regulation does not necessarily have conducive effects as many institutional investors already have a tax optimised corporate structure.

4.4.2 Market-based incentives

Our analysis also provides mixed evidence for market based incentives such as emission trading schemes and green certificate schemes on subsequent RE investments. GHG emission trading systems have been introduced in the US, Australia, UK, Italy and Norway since 1991. First, aggregated results as well as sectoral results from the wind and biomass sectors highlight the robust positive influence of tradable permit systems. This might be due to the fact that wind energy can be installed in relevant capacities and biomass plants generate a constant flow of certificate an exhibit base-load characteristics. We thereby confirm earlier literature on GHG systems (Helm, 2002; Quirion, 2010; Rogge & Hoffmann, 2010; Rogge et al., 2011; S. Smith & Swierzbinski, 2007).

Interestingly, the presence of GHG emissions allowances have a stronger impact on the capacity financed by institutional investors than FIT, as investors prefer market-based systems which are less dependent on policy changes which is the case in aggregated results and the wind and biomass sectors. Our results add empirical evidence to the debate revolving around FITs and tradable permits (Butler & Neuhoff, 2008; Cansino et al., 2010).

On the other hand, GHG emissions allowances show a negative impact on the capacity financed by institutional investors in the solar sector. Solar energy technologies, being less mature, cost-effective and more diverse than wind, are more heavily dependent on regulation, although grid parity is almost reached. These developments are reflected in our results regarding the policy mix. Market based incentives (such as GHG emission trading systems) prove to be ineffective in this case. A possible explanation lies in the fact, that solar technologies require stronger signals towards investors due to their relative novelty compared to wind technologies. We thereby confirm Johnstone et al. (2010a) who found that market based approaches favour technologies (such as wind) that are closer to competitiveness with fossil fuels whereas feed-in tariffs are conducive to innovation in less mature technologies (such as solar).

Second, green certificates that permit trading the obligatory RE capacity in a national scheme do not incentivise institutional investors to install more solar capacity which might be due to the lack in maturity and the low amount of certificates generated per capital invested compared to other sectors, such as wind. These measures depend on the total quantity in the market which might vary resulting in insufficient mobilisation of funds and high regulatory uncertainty. In addition, quota-based systems tend to be opaque as they involve over-the-counter transactions for certificates (Cárdenas-Rodríguez et al., 2013). Our results contrast Szabó and Jäger-Waldau (2008) as well as Jensen and Skytte (2002) who conceptualised a positive influence of these renewable certificate markets. In sum, institutional investors like the openness of market based policy measures, as long as they promise reliable support for their investments (Chassot et al., 2014). Possible risks through technological or natural uncertainties lead to hard to calculate returns which lower the appetite for investments into RE.

Independent variables (ANPM) (t-1)	Overview							
	Multiple RE		Wind		Solar		Biomass	
	PCSE	OLS	PCSE	OLS	PCSE	OLS	PCSE	OLS
$EI\_FI\_FI_{jk}$	+ (***)	+ (**)	+ (**)	+ (***)	+ (***)	+ (***)	+ (NS)	+ (NS)
$EI\_FI\_GS_{jk}$	+ (NS)	+ (NS)	+ (NS)	+ (NS)	+ (***)	+ (**)	+ (**)	+ (**)
$EI\_FI\_L_{jk}$	- (NS)	- (NS)	+ (NS)	+ (NS)	- (***)	- (**)	- (NS)	- (NS)
$EI\_FI\_TR_{jk}$	+ (**)	+ (NS)	+ (NS)	+ (NS)	- (NS)	- (NS)	+ (NS)	+ (NS)
$EI\_FI\_T_{jk}$	- (*)	- (*)	- (NS)	- (NS)	+ (**)	+ (*)	- (NS)	- (NS)
$EI\_MI\_GA_{jk}$	+ (**)	+ (**)	+ (***)	+ (***)	- (**)	- (NS)	+ (*)	+ (NS)
$EI\_MI\_GC_{jk}$	- (NS)	- (NS)	- (NS)	- (NS)	- (***)	- (***)	+ (NS)	+ (NS)
$EI\_DI\_FSG_{jk}$	- (*)	- (NS)	- (NS)	- (NS)	- (***)	- (***)	+ (***)	+ (***)
$EI\_DI\_II_{jk}$	+ (NS)	+ (NS)	+ (NS)	+ (NS)	+ (NS)	+ (NS)	- (**)	- (***)
PS_IC_{jk}	- (NS)	- (NS)	+ (NS)	+ (NS)	- (***)	- (NS)	+ (**)	+ (**)
PS_SP_{jk}	+ (*)	+ (**)	+ (NS)	+ (NS)	+ (***)	+ (***)	- (*)	- (NS)
RI_CS_{jk}	+ (***)	+ (NS)	+ (**)	+ (**)	+ (**)	+ (NS)	- (NS)	- (NS)
RI_OS_{jk}	+ (NS)	+ (NS)	- (NS)	- (NS)	+ (NS)	+ (NS)	- (NS)	- (NS)
RI_MR_{jk}	+ (NS)	+ (NS)	+ (NS)	+ (NS)	+ (**)	+ (*)	+ (NS)	+ (NS)
Control variables								
c_TEC_{jk}	+ (NS)	+ (***)	+ (***)	+ (***)	+ (NS)	+ (NS)	- (***)	- (***)
c_CI_{jk}	- (NS)	- (NS)	+ (**)	+ (NS)	- (***)	- (**)	+ (***)	+ (***)
c_LIR_{jk}	- (***)	- (***)	- (***)	- (***)	- (NS)	- (NS)	- (**)	- (*)
c_SP_{jk}	+ (***)	+ (***)	+ (***)	+ (***)	- (NS)	- (NS)	+ (NS)	+ (*)
c_GDP_{jk}	- (NS)	- (NS)	- (NS)	- (NS)	- (NS)	- (NS)	+ (***)	+ (***)
_cons	- (**)	- (***)	- (**)	- (***)	+ (NS)	+ (NS)	- (***)	- (***)
R^2	0.38	0.38	0.40	0.40	0.49	0.49	0.38	0.38

***, **, *, denote significance at 1, 5 and 10% significance levels, respectively;
NS refers to 'not statistically significant'.

Table 12 – Overview about the results

4.4.3 Direct investments

According to our results from the biomass sector positive contributions with high significance include funds to sub-national governments (direct investments of federal money with regional, local or municipal level entities as intermediaries or targets) as biomass markets tend to be regionally dispersed. We hereby confirm earlier works (based on wind sector analyses) which highlighted that this form of direct investment spurs RE deployment (Bird et al., 2005; De Jager et al., 2008; Menz & Vachon, 2006; Ragwitz et al., 2008). Our results from the solar sector revealed that this type of instrument is ineffective in promoting solar capacity addition. This might be due to the fact that institutional investors ignore subsidies on a local level.

Infrastructure investments to provide grid access seem ineffective for channelling investor's money into biomass technologies. This stands in contrast to previous literature which highlights the grid expansion as conducive to RE deployment and investment (De Jager et al., 2011; Henriot, 2013; Steinbach, 2013). Reasons for deviating results in the biomass energy sector (compared to solar and wind) lie in the different structure which can be characterised by a strong regional focus and usually the small scale of power plants (Upreti, 2004). This might attract a different set of investors that focus less on overall market conditions.

4.4.4 Policy support

When examining the influence of policy support measures on subsequent investments into RE capacity, our results show interesting characteristics. First, institutional creation, such as the forming an energy agency, accelerates the capacity additions in the biomass sector effectively. On the other hand, results from the solar sector show the contrary. A possible explanation lies in the fact that the sudden cut in the Spanish feed-in tariff system is coded as an institutional creation/change.

Secondly, aggregated and solar sector results show that a clear long-term energy strategy (strategic planning) is conducive to investments as investors favour a long-term framework with a clear vision. Essentially, all countries in our study had policy measures containing a strategic component, however only a few incorporated it in many policy initiatives.

With this analysis, we add empirical support for the strong role which a long-term policy commitment (strategic planning) plays in an effective policy mix. De Jager et al. (2011) state that commitment, stability, reliability and predictability are all elements that increase confidence of market actors, reduce regulatory risks, and hence significantly reduce cost of capital. Additional evidence points towards a preference for policy consistency even when changes occur (W. White et al., 2013). Thus, our results confirm conceptual and empirical works by several scholars, which hold clear strategic long-term economic instruments to be conducive to RE investments (Lüthi & Wüstenhagen, 2012b; W. White et al., 2013; Wüstenhagen & Menichetti, 2012). Finally, we confirm work by Marques and Fuinhas (2012a) who highlight the policy processes and strategy frameworks as positive for RE deployment. Possible risks through instability in regulation directly affect investors' return calculations and determine investment decisions immediately (Wüstenhagen & Menichetti, 2012). Therefore, a long-term vision for the regulatory environment through strategic planning and most likely through institutional creation will support the investment environment for institutional investors.

4.4.5 Regulatory instruments

Regulatory mechanisms and institutionalisation of markets in the form of codes and standards (especially RPS) also attract institutional investors. According to our results this is the case for the aggregated sectors as well as in the wind sector, perhaps because the wind sector shows elements of a developed market based on mature technologies. The cost-effectiveness of this technology is proven, so it can compete with fossil fuel-based electricity generation in certain environments.

We also provide new insights in the discussion about RPS schemes. Looking at US states, Carley (2009) found a positive effect, whereas Delmas and Montes-Sancho (2011) did not find a significant positive contribution of RPS to RE investments. Thus, we confirm Carley (2009), Bird et al. (2005), and Menz & Vachon (2006) for a sample of countries beyond the USA. On the other hand, we contrast Delmas & Montes-Sancho (2011). Reliable support through codes and standards or obligation schemes supports investments into RE through institutional investors. These policy measures are mostly long term and not easily retractable, so it gives them certainty in their investment calculations.

4.4.6 Robustness checks

We performed a number of robustness checks to verify the stability of our results. First of all we estimated pooled OLS regressions (which have the strongest assumptions with regard to heteroskedasticy and auto-correlation as well as distribution of errors) and calculated the variance inflation factors (VIF). The analysis revealed that only in the model for the solar sector, multi-collinearity might be an issue (mean of VIF 9.17). However, this high value stems from the VIF of our control variables and therefore has no influence on the coefficients of our independent variables of interest (i.e. the policy measures). Second, we estimated random effects estimators (REE) for our models (see Table 20 in the appendix). All our models (PCSE, OLS and REE) display consistent results. When using the OLS model, grants and subsidies as well as codes and standards become insignificant. Third, we ran our models, including only the significant variables from our previous analysis. These analysis displayed consistent results throughout all models. Finally, to account for the excessive number of zeros in our sample, we crosschecked the disaggregated results (i.e. individual policy instruments) with aggregated results (categories of policy instruments) for the entire analysis. The models displayed consistent results.

4.5 Conclusions and policy implications

This work contributes to two different streams of the academic literature: Exploring the effectiveness of RE policies as well as observing the role of policies in the decision making process for RE capacity investments through institutional investors. Our research revealed mixed evidence from the wind, solar and biomass sector. We call for technology specific policies, taking into account the actual market conditions and the position in the technology life cycle to design a supportive policy mix. Our results strongly suggest the establishment of a reliable framework with a clear vision and long-term policy objectives regarding the RE capacities to be installed in the future as well as complementary transitions in the energy sector. Ex-post changes to the remuneration of existing projects should be avoided. However, as technological progress continues, the measures taken need to be adjusted, taking the market and technological conditions (i.e. life cycle) into account.

Within this framework, monetary and fiscal and economic incentives are the most relevant policy measures for investors. These directly impact the risk/return profile of RE projects and, thus, their attractiveness. Investors are positive about long-term reliable support mechanisms that cannot be revoked and provide a highly predictable revenue stream. FIT provide more reliable and long-term signal than grants which depend on public budgets. However these funds influence the direct and early project cash flows, which is also seen favourable.

According to our results, market based incentives (such as GHG emission trading systems) can also have strong influence on investments by institutional investors. These measures support the need of investors for a highly reliable environment, best accompanied by a diminished risk exposure. However, for an emission trading system to become an effective anchor for institutional investors, the technology deployed should have reached maturity.

Supportive regulatory measures such as codes and standards (especially RPS) accelerate the diffusion process of RE technologies by further reducing technological and regulatory risk associated with investments in RE projects. Thus we recommend the streamlining and strengthening of legislation and a transparent setting of renewable energy targets.

Our results also provide implications for institutional RE investors who are looking for stable returns unrelated to volatile capital markets. They recognize a regulatory environment which supports their investments or lowers their risks. We suggest them to allocate their funds in countries which have shown to be long-term supporters of the RE markets and have not changed policies abruptly. Higher certainty in the reliability of RE technologies and increasing cost competitiveness make the market increasingly independent from direct support mechanisms. To accelerate the further diffusion the policy focus can move towards a reliable environment for RE.

There are a number of limitations regarding study design and modelling. First, the use of dummy variables for the policy measures does not allow for statements concerning policy implementation, policy design or policy uncertainty (Bergek et al., 2013a; Jenner et al., 2013; Lüthi & Wüstenhagen, 2012b; Müller et al., 2011). Second, our analysis does not cover the most recent developments in RE deployment and investments (2012 onwards) due to data availability.

Amending our fine grained policy analysis, future studies could look at the influence of these and other policies on general capacity additions among different types of private and institutional investors such as banks, insurances, university endowments, pension funds and family offices as well as including non-institutional investments such as households and utilities. Furthermore, interaction effects between the different policy instruments are worthwhile investigating in a longitudinal research design to discover complementarities and synergies. Geographically our research could be extended to the BRIC countries and less developed countries (LDC) which might alter the results due to an different institutional setting (Friebe et al., 2013, 2014). Finally, it would be interesting to close the link between early stage and later stage financing along the finance value chain for RE technologies, thus analysing the support environment for venture capital and private equity investments in the early and later stages of RE companies which might interact with RE project investments.

4.6 Acknowledgements

The authors are grateful for the time and support of Martin Kenney, Donald Patton (University of California, Davis), Alex Coad, and Paul Nightingale (SPRU – University of Sussex). We thank six anonymous reviewers for useful comments and suggestions. In addition the discussion at the ZEW Energy Conference 2014 helped us in further refining our arguments. We would like to thank the Federal Ministry of Education and Research (BMBF), Germany, for their financial support as part of the research project ''Climate Change, Financial Markets and Innovation (CFI)''.

5 Development of Industries in the Cleantech Sector - A Case of the Solar and Fuel Cell Industries

Authors: Michael Migendt, Florian A. Täube, Brett A. Gilbert & Paschen von Flotow

Abstract:

This paper presents in a condensed view the role of finance, innovation, and policy for the development of cleantech industries: It explains the historical development of the solar energy and fuel cell industries and depicts the peculiarities of green growth. A quantitative content analysis of press articles from American newspapers is used to analyze the changing importance of different topics during the period from 1995 to 2013. An approach to compare the importance of the different actors, finance, innovation, and policy has been recognized as missing in the literature. This paper adds not only to the theoretical research gap, but it also a new methodological approach within industry development literature. Finance as a key barrier to green growth is shown to be of high importance even before investment readiness. Innovation themes are discovered to be of higher importance than entrepreneurial themes during the earlier phases of industry development. Additionally, the solar energy industry is under higher regulatory influence compared to the fuel cell industry.

5.1 Introduction

Many clean technologies have reached market maturity. Nowadays, most of the applications of common technologies, like wind and solar for energy generation, smart energy usage in the energy efficiency field or electric cars and fuel cells in mobility, are accepted in the market place and find use in a variety of product solutions. Still there are barriers to overcome to reach a higher market share (Altenburg & Pegels, 2012; Foxon & Pearson, 2008b). The development of mature green industries might be used as a benchmark for new emerging industries, thus the historical tale of the development of industries is of high value. Especially in the rapidly growing field of green innovation, the demand of a re-assessment of technological change and industry development is high (Markard et al., 2012; A. Smith et al., 2010).

The development path of industries and connected technologies is in general of high interest for entrepreneurs, managers, policy makers and academics. Following industry development has been of major interest in scholarly research, in fact, several scholars have researched the key factors driving the emergence and legitimization of industries.

Industry and technology development literature often research the relationship of single actors to economic and industry growth, but neglect the reciprocity of the different actors active in the process. Viewpoints from several disciplines should be taken into account to consider the importance of economics, entrepreneurship, finance, policy and innovation studies (Aghion et al., 2009; Autio et al., 2014; Geels, 2014; Levine, 2005; Mazzucato, 2013a; Miller & Garnsey, 2000).

Finance, innovation and policy have been recognized as important for growth of industries. Nonetheless, the role and importance of these actors in a comparative setting remains an under researched area (Audretsch, 1995; Dosi, 1990; Florida & Kenney, 1988b; Soskice, 1997). A quantitative content analysis of press articles from the United States is used in this paper to analyze and describe the historical development of selected clean technology industries. The results of the software backed analysis allows for a new comparative approach to explain the role and importance of finance, innovation, and policy (Migendt, Täube, Gilbert, & von Flotow, 2014; Phillips et al., 2004; Ventresca & Mohr, 2002; Wuthnow, 1989). Finance topics are generally of high importance and get the most attention even before the industry reaches peak investment activity. Technology and innovation issues are of higher importance in earlier development phases, while regulation topics get more attention in later phases. Unexpectedly, entrepreneurship topics associated with the founder or founding process are not important in the beginning, but rather gain importance over time.

The main research question of this paper is:

What role do innovation, investments and policy play in the development of (cleantech) industries?

Section 5.2 briefly describes the conceptual motivation and provides a literature overview. Section 5.3 introduces the data and methodology used. Section 5.4 presents the results and discussion, while Section 5.5 ends with a conclusion, limitations and further possibilities for research.

5.2 Theoretical framework

Transitions toward sustainable industries are a relatively recent phenomenon. Several industries like the energy and mobility industries have changed or are currently changing towards less resource usage and less carbon emissions. These shifts within innovation systems affect socio-technical configurations, as well as, active institutions. Multi-actor interactions play a key role in this development (Coenen, Benneworth, &

Truffer, 2012; Farla et al., 2012; Geels, 2014; Markard et al., 2012; A. Smith et al., 2010).

Sustainable innovation has developed and will develop along technological pathways that are dependent on societal preferences and thus have to be attractive for all stakeholders. Green innovation is at the heart of this process. However, it has its peculiarities. Especially the role of regulation and policy plays a more important factor for the development of these innovations and connected industries (Altenburg & Pegels, 2012; Foxon & Pearson, 2008b; Jacobsson & Bergek, 2004).

Comparative approaches analyzing the role of finance, innovation, and policy in industry evolution are rare. This paper looks at this phenomenon from three different perspectives:

Firstly, finance has been recognized as a highly important factor for innovation in industries and following industry growth by Schumpeter (1934, 1942). Recently new works have shed light on the more specific role of finance, intermediaries and risk capital for industry growth (Mazzucato, 2013a; Mina et al., 2013). "Financial dynamics differ not only between sectors, and between phases in an industry's life-cycle, but also over longer phases of technological revolutions" (Mazzucato, 2013a, p. 353). No access to finance constitutes a huge barrier not only for young innovative firms, but also later in their development cycle. Still there is a broad spectrum of financing alternatives for the companies. Private equity and venture capital finance play a role especially in the earlier growth phases of firms, and are thus highly important to industry emergence (Berger & Udell, 1998; Florida & Kenney, 1988b; Mina et al., 2013).

Secondly, innovative firms are the drivers of industry development, while, surprisingly, pure innovation is not the origin of growth. The need for an institutional system and a guiding policy framework are an often mentioned prerequisite for a prosperous economy (Audretsch, 1995; Fagerberg & Verspagen, 2002; Mazzucato & Perez, 2014; Soskice, 1997; H. Van de Ven, 1993). Entrepreneurship is key to new industries and their growth. Founding activity is an important component in early entrepreneurial ecosystems and over time entrepreneurs are important for steering companies through the diverse development phases. Their role for building legitimacy is central for emerging industries. Entrepreneurs are seen as agents of change that "can play a defining role in the technology's diffusion by launching it in the market place, making it available for adoption, and subsequently managing the growth of a firm around it" (Miller & Garnsey, 2000, p. 461). Notably, their role is seen as more important in earlier phases of a technology life-cycle (Aldrich & Fiol, 1994; Autio et al., 2014; Déjean, Gond, & Leca, 2004; Miller & Garnsey, 2000).

Thirdly, technology and innovation policy play an important role for economic growth and industry development. Policy has to be adjusted to the stages in the innovation cycle and has always influenced the growth in the respective phases. The term 'policy-mix' describes the interactions and interdependencies between different policies and has been used to explain the complexity of today's regulatory environment (Aghion et al., 2009; Borrás & Edquist, 2013; Flanagan et al., 2011a).

Having laid out the theoretical lenses of the three different actors, finance, innovation, and policy, which support industry development, this paper builds on the descriptions of emerging green innovations & industries (for a literature overview on green innovation development see Schiederig, Tietze, & Herstatt, 2012). To extend the scope of the analysis it adds technology aspects and entrepreneurship to the actor innovation and venture capital to the actor finance (Garud & Karnøe, 2003; Godoe & Nygaard, 2006; Hall & Kerr, 2003; Hellman & van den Hoed, 2007; Hendry & Harborne, 2011; Jacobsson & Bergek, 2004; Negro & Hekkert, 2008; A. H. Van de Ven & Garud, 1991).

5.3 Research methodology & data

5.3.1 Cases of industry evolution

Adopting a case narrative, this paper observes the solar energy and fuel cell industries. These industries are both seen as core to the clean technology sector but still have different characteristics. They target different markets, have to face different regulatory settings, emerged at different points in time, and have different technological backgrounds.

Solar energy represents the first case: Light and heat created by the sun can be used as solar energy through various technologies. First, there is solar photovoltaic (PV), which generates electric energy and second, there is solar thermal, which generates heat energy. Solar PV converts light directly into electricity. It is composed of semiconductor cells assembled into solar modules, which together build a solar system. Solar thermal is used to generate heat. This heat can be used to generate electricity, nonetheless, but solar thermal energy has captured just a quite small fraction of the overall market. The solar PV energy industry emerged out of technological innovations for space exploration, and by the 1970s found some application in off-grid use and started initial commercial sales for home or industry use in the early 1990s. The market size was negligibly small with shipments of systems with 71.5 MWp in 1995 growing to 252 MWp in 2000, 1407 MWp in 2005, 17.4 GWp in 2010 leading to 39 GWp in 2013. Production of solar PV systems now mostly takes place in China and Taiwan, while a lot of the installations take place in Europe and the US (Fraunhofer ISE, 2014; Mints, 2006; NREL, 2011).

The second case is the fuel cell industry: Fuel cells convert chemical energy from fuels, like hydrogen or methane, through a chemical reaction with oxygen to electricity. They consist of an anode, a cathode and differing electrolytes. These electrolytes are what mainly distinguish the types of fuel cells. Fuel cells can be used in transportation or other portable power applications or also in stationary settings. They are seen as clean, energy-efficient and do not necessarily emit emissions at the point of operation. The market has grown consistently reaching 35,000 units in 2013. 30,000 thereof in a stationary application (Hall & Kerr, 2003; Hellman & van den Hoed, 2007; Satyapal, 2014; Steele & Heinzel, 2001; U.S. Department of Energy, 2014).

5.3.2 Data

This paper builds on self-assembled dataset to gain a picture of the historical development of clean technology industries. The database consists of press publications from major American newspapers from the timeframe from January 1st,1995 to December 31st, 2013. Source for the articles is the Lexis Nexis database with its records of press and company publications. The data was compiled of seven of the top ten US newspapers, which were available through Lexis Nexis. The majority of articles stem from the New York Times, Washington Post and the San Jose Mercury News.

As key search terms for the solar industry the term "solar energy" was used. For the fuel cell industry the term "fuel cell" was used. Resulting for the solar industry the database returned 3,659 articles and for the fuel cell industry 1,697 articles.

Additionally to the media analysis, further information was derived from the Thomson One Banker database of private equity investments. The investment data used is from the years 1995 until 2013. This data shows the amount invested and the number of deals in the respective solar energy and fuel cell industry. The investments are split according to the investment stages. The stages are separated according to seed, early, expansion and late stage investments.

5.3.3 Method

A quantitative content analysis of press articles is used in this paper to analyze and describe the historical development of clean technology industries. This method has been used in different contexts and disciplines lately (Migendt et al., 2014; Phillips et al., 2004; Ventresca & Mohr, 2002; Wuthnow, 1989). The approach used allows for a deep, but still unbiased assessment of large quantities of data. The quality of the information depends not only on the textual sources, but also on the process of the software guided analysis (Berelson, 1952; Elo & Kyngäs, 2007; R. P. Weber, 1990). A lesser quantitative approach then in this paper has been used to assess the system functions in innovation systems in the German biomass digestion industry (Negro & Hekkert, 2008). This paper uses WordStat 6.0 by Provalis Research to analyze the article database. Wordstat is a commercial software package used for content analysis and text mining in unstructured textual documents. WordStat analyzes texts and structures results according to dictionaries. These dictionaries consist of words grouped in thematic clusters, which are then processed through the software. The software is able to recognize the occurrence of single words or word clusters as well as relations (Krippendorff, 2012; Neuendorf, 2002). To describe the development of the different industries two separate, but still related dictionaries were developed. The main structure of the word clusters was equal, just the technology frame differs between the sectors (see dictionaries in the appendix). The dictionary was built according to the actors finance, innovation, and policy, with additional sub-actors in entrepreneurship and venture capital. Industry specific technology themes have been added as additional actors, as well. The words and word groups creating the dictionaries were developed in a deductive way. The deductive approach, also called top-down or directed approach is based on existing frameworks or theory to derive categories and included topics. An already existing reference is used to analyze textual information. In this paper the dictionaries include words and word groups based on the actors and actors' synonyms as well as key topics associated with the main actors. For example, the sub-actor "ENTREPRENEURSHIP" consists of words based on the root word "ENTREPR*" (the * signals a flexible ending of a word) and the words "FOUNDER", "STARTUP" and "START-UP" Additionally to the actors and sub-actors, the technology actor consists in the solar energy sector dictionary of solar energy technology, photovoltaic and thermal. Respectively, in the fuel cell sector dictionary consists of the different basic materials for fuel cells: alkaline, molten carbonate, phosphoric acid, proton exchange membrane, solid oxide and zinc air (Elo & Kyngäs, 2007; Hsieh & Shannon, 2005; R. P. Weber, 1990). The approach used can best be described as summative content analysis. The goal is to explore usage of words and interpret it with help of further information. In the course of the analysis the occurrence of these actors and sub-actors can be tracked. In the following paragraph, the relative importance of the actors is analyzed over time and compared to the others. Mirroring the press articles on the technologies with the corresponding investment data enriches the results (Boykoff, 2008; Hsieh & Shannon, 2005).

5.4 Results and discussion

Using a comparative case narrative this paper contrasts the results of the solar energy and fuel cell industry. The industries, which have both reached certain market acceptance today developed to their prominence not only in the market place, but also in the investment area and in media attention. The overall media attention towards these industries has been very volatile. While fuel cell had its peak of attention in 2003, it has lost a lot of the media coverage since, while the solar energy industry had its peak in 2012. This pattern coincides with the deal activity in these industries. The correlation between deal activity and articles in the "solar energy" field is approximately 0.90 and in the "fuel cell" field reaches approximately 0.54.

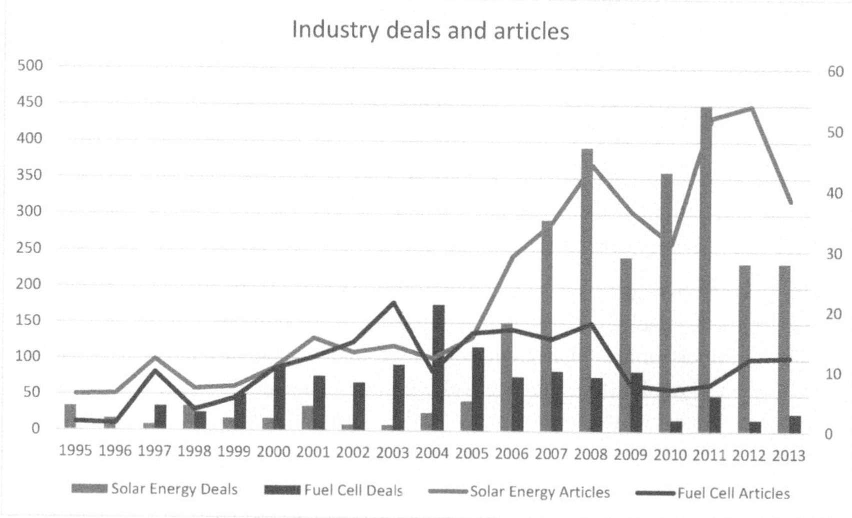

Figure 16 – Industry deals and article

	Solar Energy Articles	*Solar Energy Deals*	*Fuel Cell Articles*	*Fuel Cell Deals*
Solar Energy Articles	1			
Solar Energy Deals	0,8995	1		
Fuel Cell Articles	-0,1430	-0,0797	1	
Fuel Cell Deals	0,1369	0,3162	0,5353	1

Table 13 – Correlation table article & investments

Articles reporting on solar energy cover a broad spectrum of topics. All actors included in our dictionary get some attention over time. Particularly important are finance and regulation topics, which are covered on average in 45 % or 44 % of all articles. Entrepreneurship gets attention in 13 % of the articles, while innovation gets 11 %. Venture capital only reaches 5 % of the coverage.

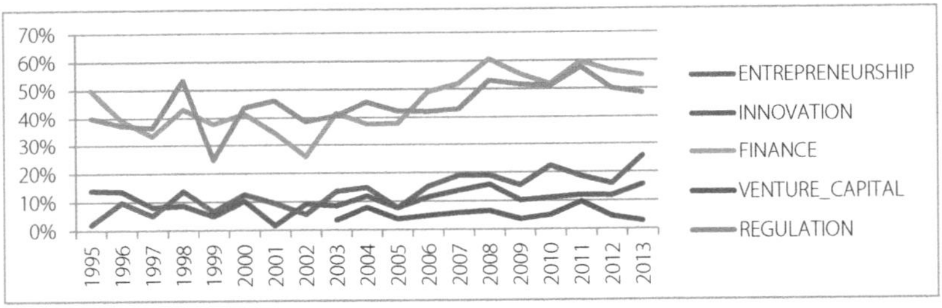

Figure 17 – Sector frames „solar energy“

Similar to solar energy all actors and sub-actors from the dictionaries get attention in the fuel cell article subset. Even the average attention resembles that of solar energy. Still highly important are finance and regulation topics which are covered on average in 40 % or 34 % of all articles respectively. Entrepreneurship coverage lies at 14 % of the articles, while innovation lies at 12 %. VC gets 5 % of the attention. The most significant difference appears on regulation reporting. The solar energy industry as part of the power sector is by nature under heavier regulatory influence, thus explaining this gap.

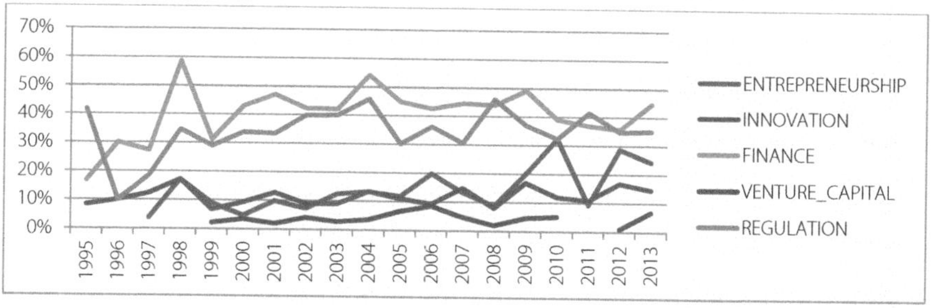

Figure 18 – Sector frames "fuel cell"

Looking at the development of the attention towards actors it is possible to observe the changing importance of those during industry growth. The peak of investments coincides with the peaks in media attention towards finance. This shows the clear connection of reporting on deal activity. Reporting on venture capital nevertheless started only in 2003, after early investments already had already taken place, but before a more established investment area emerged. Venture capital articles even precede real deal activity. This might be due to the lemmings phenomena VCs often have to face. VCs are often blamed for only investing in new topics if others already have already taken the lead and a topic has gained certain attention, including media attention (Cheng, 2009; Haislip, 2010; Lacy, 2008). Innovation reporting starts with relatively high relevance from the beginning, while entrepreneurship topics only start after the start of a more active investment environment. Articles on regulation and policy start quite late as well, as they are a signal of a maturing industry. Comparing the results of the solar energy and fuel cell sector, it is possible to observe that the importance of regulation is on average higher in the solar energy sector. The growth of this industry has been fueled by public interventions and support mechanisms typical for the power sector. Some solar companies profited heavily from state subsidies or guarantees. The other four actors have fluctuating importance, but get on average the same attention over the years.

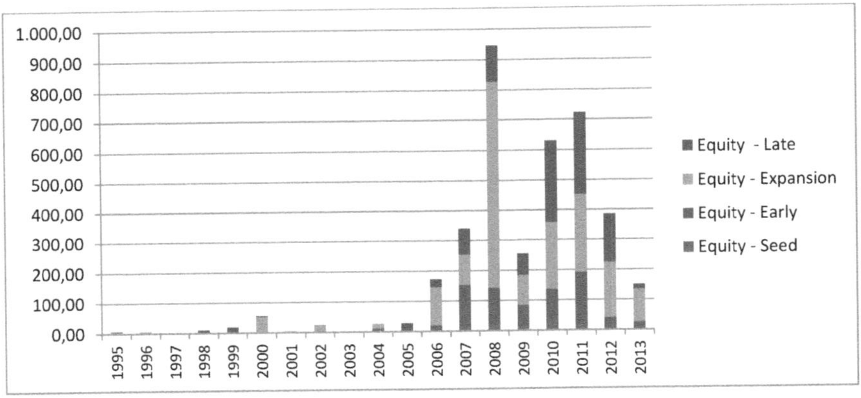

Figure 19 – Investment stage funding "solar energy" (in mUSD)

Investments in the solar industry started as early as 1995 in our analysis. Much of the deal activity started eleven years later in 2006. The growth in the following two years was significant. The invested sums peaked in 2008 and dropped drastically during the financial crisis. Recovering investment activity in the years 2010 and 2011, followed by a change to later stage rounds since then speaks to a mature industry not exposed to many new entrants. The fuel cell industry had reached most deal activity in 2004 and most funds invested in 2006. No drop can be recognized after the start of the financial crisis as most VC investments shifted to late stage deals in recent years. This shows that these investments are follow-on investments. Fuel cell might therefore get defined as an already fairly mature industry. This is true to the extent that the industry has not seen many new entrants in recent years and that a consolidation of market forces took place a while ago. Still the technologies are changing and no dominant technology has yet manifested, which speaks to a less mature industry than solar energy technology.

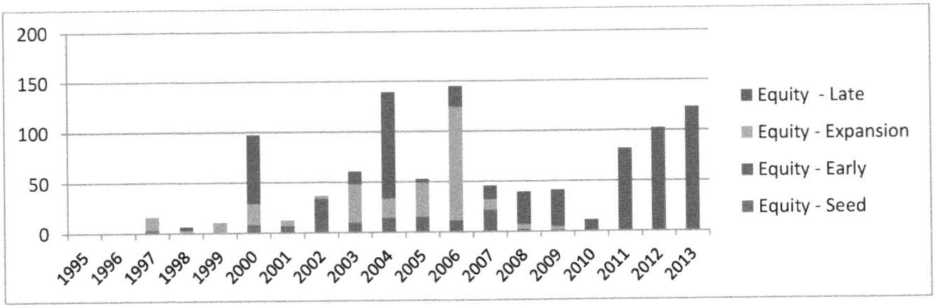

Figure 20 – Investment stage funding "fuel cell" (in mUSD)

This paper analyzed additionally to the actors the specifics of the technologies. In general it is interesting to observe that the kind of media used in this research, namely mainstream daily newspapers, rarely reports on the technology details of the industries regarded in this paper. The solar energy industry with "not very specific technology vocabulary" reaches a maximum of approximately a quarter of the articles mentioning solar energy technology specifics. In fuel cell sector news very few technology topics get mentioned with a maximum of 15 % on one kind of fuel cell type. The reporting on solid oxide fuel cells (SOFC) is heavily influenced by articles on Bloom Energy, a successful VC financed company using this technology (see Figure 24 in the appendix).

5.5 Concluding remarks

This paper uses a case narrative on two clean technology industries to observe the industry development through the lenses of the actors finance, innovation, and policy. The clean technology industries "solar energy" and "fuel cell" developed over the last decades and have reached a certain level of technology, as well as, market maturity. Solar energy is a more mature industry even as media attention and VC investment activity started later and peaked later. New innovations continue to emerge from these industries, but additional barriers in the development process have to be surpassed. The most important actors in media development of these industries prove to be finance and regulation with innovation lagging behind. This paper sheds light on the need for a comparative analysis of these actors and depicts their role for industry development and the transition towards a more sustainable economy (Markard et al., 2012; A. Smith et al., 2010).

Green innovation peculiarities lead to the demand of a re-assessment of technological change and industry development. Contrasting to previous research the results of this paper show that the role of readiness for financial market is important for investments and the growth of an industry. Entrepreneurship, which most often is mentioned as a prerequisite for the emergence of an industry and in the earliest phases of company formation, plays a less important role in the eye of the media. The attention towards this topic grows in later phases of industry development. More important in earlier phases are technological and innovation themes. This late entry of entrepreneurship is possibly different than in other industries, like web or software, which are driven by human capital and less so by technology. The two regarded industries do not only show green innovation specifics, but also prove to be different. Solar energy as part of the power sector shows a very high importance of regulatory topics compared to the fuel cell industry (Audretsch, 1995; Dosi, 1990; Florida & Kenney, 1988b; Soskice, 1997).

This paper has, as all research does, some empirical and methodological limitations. It uses a regional subset of the industries, and given the focus on US examples lacks some important regions of development. In solar energy especially Germany and China play an important role in shaping the market place, while in the fuel cell industry some European and Canadian firms have been drivers of the development. The quantitative content analysis can be inattentive to the broader meaning of the textual information and relies on the credibility of the dictionary which can be addressed through internal consistency (Hsieh & Shannon, 2005). Importance and interactions of finance, innovation and policy as drivers for industry development need further research. A more quantified approach could help to explain the role of these topics in more detail.

Key implications for policy makers and managers are that the rightly adjusted attention towards topics at the right point in life-cycle development helps to understand the growth trajectories of an industry. Thus, observing media is a possible way to recognize industry maturity and possible legitimacy of technologies. Market entry decisions, expansion plans from entrepreneurs and managers can be based on these results. An effect of media attention on policy measures or investment decisions might occur, but through this industry level approach not all possibilities are provable. Still, establishing a supporting regulatory framework earlier in the development could lead to lower barriers for financing new technologies.

Future research could build on this methodology and compare further industries. Contrasting industries with more differences than the clean technology industries considered here could show more variety in the role of the actors for industry development.

6 Conclusion

The goal of this dissertation was to explore examples of alternative investments in the field of clean technologies. It considers venture capital, private equity, and infrastructure asset classes and a broad range of green industries, as well as, suitable policy approaches to accelerate green innovation. Four studies address the field with different methodological approaches and from different viewpoints. This chapter summarizes the findings and implications across all studies and presents a concise synopsis:

6.1 Accelerating green innovation through alternative investments

Accelerating green innovation through alternative investments is of high importance to strengthen the transition to a sustainable economy. Chapter 2 set the stage to describe the emergence of the cleantech VC investment category. It developed a venture capital life-cycle model and described the role of finance and policy for the transition towards sustainability (Avnimelech & Teubal, 2006; Markard et al., 2012; Penna & Geels, 2012). In addition it proved the significance of finance in the innovation field by showing the high influence of VC and VC's investors on key turning points in industry emergence on accelerating green innovation (Kenney, 2011a; Mazzucato, 2013a; Wonglimpiyarat, 2011; Mina et al., 2013). Chapter 2 added a systemic perspective on the industry emergence to the research debate and recognized historical drivers, which accelerated green innovation.

Building on these results, chapter 3 extended the relevance of the finance sector for innovation. The exploratory interview based study showed how the whole "innovation finance value chain", including institutional investors, VC/PE investors, and innovators, plays a role for green innovation (Kenney, 2011a; Wonglimpiyarat, 2011; Perez, 2002a; Hekkert et al., 2007; Johnson, 2001). Effects in innovation that do not accelerate but retard green innovation are unintended consequences and negative feedback effects, which happened between financial policy and innovation policy in the clean technology sector. These effects led to growing barriers to finance and thus less green innovation (Lovio, Mickwitz, & Heiskanen, 2011; Mazzucato, 2000; Peneder, 2010). Additionally, private investments into renewable energies are a core component of the transition to a green energy sector. The funds flowing in energy assets in OECD countries were shown in chapter 4. Most effective policy measures for the diffusion of renewables prove to be those directly impacting the return for investors. However, not only quantifiable factors induce investments but as well a reliable framework with a clear vision and long-term policy objectives are important to support renewable energies (Bergek, Mignon, & Sundberg, 2013b; Wüstenhagen & Menichetti, 2012). Chapter 5 condensed the previous results by comparing the role of finance, innovation and policy in cases of clean technology industry development. It explained the circumstances needed to attract investments to an industry and added a perspective on industry evolution in clean technologies. This contributes to the understanding of accelerating factors for green innovation (Audretsch, 1995; Dosi, 1990; Florida & Kenney, 1988b).

6.2 The changing role of finance and policy along the cleantech innovation chain

As shown from the analyses conducted in this thesis, financiers and policy makers are key actors for green innovation. The manifestation of these actors changes along the clean technology innovation chain. During the technology generation stage, both, financial and policy support are in the hand of the public. Private actors are mostly too risk averse to engage in early phases and sponsor R&D. Chapter 3 highlighted the need for public support in early stages of the development. Technology push mechanisms and public R&D funding trigger innovations that are too risky for private investors (Hargadon & Kenney, 2012; Peters et al., 2012a; Samara et al., 2012). Suddenly appearing innovation does not exist, as is shown in chapter 5 by high media attention towards finance and policy in the earliest phases. A systemic environment with these actors prevalent is necessary to initiate industry emergence (Audretsch, 1995; Fagerberg & Verspagen, 2002; Mazzucato & Perez, 2014; H. Van de Ven, 1993).

With the technology commercialization stage, private investors start to engage in innovation processes. Chapter 2 showed the changing environment of VC activity along the life-cycle stages. In conjunction with technological breakthroughs and beginning market acceptance VC funds engage in innovative companies (Avnimelech et al., 2004; Gompers & Lerner, 2001). Nevertheless investors need a reliable and transparent regulatory framework and no policy initiated negative feedback mechanisms as stated in chapter 3. Still, legislative action is needed to bridge occurring financing gaps like through the "Valley-of-Death" on the junction to the diffusion stage. Extending the roles of the actors, chapter 3 concretized the importance of finance and policy in general for green innovation (Auerswald & Branscomb, 2003; Brown, 1990; Oakey, 2003; Samila & Sorenson, 2010a).

During technology diffusion, different private financiers are active. Private equity and infrastructure investors catalyze diffusion of technologies. Chapter 2 warned to subsidize these investors to heavily at this stage to prevent overshooting and following negative feedbacks (Hargadon & Kenney, 2012; Lerner, 2002). Negative feedbacks and unintended consequences of policy are main results of chapter 3. Competing finance and innovation policy can reverse well intended goals to support green innovation (Lovio et al., 2011; Mazzucato, 2000). Chapter 4 demanded a level playing field and possibly some market pull mechanisms for the diffusion of clean technologies (Chassot et al., 2014; Johnstone, Haščič, & Popp, 2010b). In addition, heavy influence from the public should be avoided to not interfere with technology capabilities (Aghion et al., 2009; Samara et al., 2012). Chapter 5 emphasized that policy makers can chose from a variety of policy measure to support the deployment of clean technologies. Regulation conducive for late stage green innovation need to be adjusted, taking the market and technological conditions (i.e. life cycle) into account (Fischlein et al., 2010; Foxon & Pearson, 2008b; Hoppmann, 2014). All along the clean technology innovation chain chapter 5 demanded to strengthen the policy and finance actors for accelerating green innovations (Barreto & Kemp, 2007; Comin & Nanda, 2014; Foxon & Pearson, 2008b; Veugelers, 2012a).

It can be concluded based on the four studies and concrete industry and finance examples, that "[…] regulation of financial markets must go hand in hand with policies that are aimed at innovation and industrial policy" (Mazzucato, 2013a, p. 863).

6.3 Implications for investors and innovators

This thesis does not only include contributions to research but offers some insights and recommendations for action for investors and innovators. The alternative investment environment for clean technologies and renewable energies has changed rapidly over the last decades. The political will to support green innovation lead to diverse initiatives and policy interventions (Heck et al., 2014; Mowery et al., 2010a; OECD, 2011; Stern, 2006). This thesis developed an understanding of the role of investors and innovators in clean technologies and of the policy supporting environment:

Chapter 2 and chapter 5 both showed the effects of a market emergence triggered by policy support. The created green innovation led to industry growth and investment opportunities. Still, investors and innovators should act prudent in heavily regulated environments like clean technology or renewable energy. Possibilities to be impaired are various: Suddenly abolished support mechanisms, unreliable market creation regulation, overshooting markets leading to negative performance adjustments. The trend towards less capital intensive company formations in less regulated industries follows these findings. Nevertheless, as clarified in chapter 4, opportunities in regulated markets can, under transparent and reliable legislation, still be profitable in the future. It is advisable to invest or innovate in markets that have a long-term support strategy for clean technologies or renewable energies. Furthermore, technologies less reliant on policy support prove to be better suitable for private capital. Chapter 3 advises investors and innovators to keep the regulatory environment of their investors or investors' investors in mind, as changes in financial policy have through unintended negative feedback influenced innovation.

6.4 Policy implications

"Improvement of innovation performance is a long-term target that requires continuous and systematic efforts, since many policies that affect the system interrelate with the national, economic, institutional and social environment" (Samara et al., 2012, p. 637). This statement proves to be key to regulators. If they want the transition to a green economy, they have to foster green innovation. This effort has to be guided with strategic foresight and be as reliable and transparent as possible. Several policy measures have proven to be conducive to green technologies. A suitable policy mix which is not leading to overshooting or contradicting results is the goal for accelerating green innovation (Flanagan et al., 2011a; Lerner, 2002).

Chapter 2 suggests to observe phenomena that have direct influence on market growth. Policy measures connected with the right communication strategy can induce private capital and start entrepreneurial activity. The "Green Wave Initiative" of California's public pension system led to the emergence of a prosperous clean technology industry connected with innovation and job creation (nonetheless, the initiative's specific configuration might have contributed to overshooting phenomenon). Understanding and thoughtful regulation of private capital markets is thus needed to accelerate green innovation.

Chapter 3 recommends policy makers to obtain a holistic and informed view of the actors and interactions in the regulated green innovation field. Conflicting objectives between innovation policy and finance policy have to be balanced. Imbalanced and competing economic-political targets have to be prevented. The goal to stabilize the financial market in the aftermath of the financial crisis was in contrast to the goal of accelerating green innovation. Thus, prioritization of goals and possible exclusion of adversely affected competing policy targets can help to save welfare losses. Exemptive provisions for risk capital providers during the downturn could have saved the clean technology industry or prevent needed public stimulus packages. In addition, an informed perspective in regard to demand/supply characteristics of supported industries when engaging in the decision-making process for support programs could prevent from oversupply or underfunding. Oversupply of funding or support may lead to overshooting – meaning a boom market with a subsequent drastic downturn or market downturns.

The findings of chapter 4 demand technology specific policies, taking into account the actual market conditions and the position of the technology in the technology life-cycle.

The most relevant policy measures for investors are monetary/fiscal and economic incentives. These directly impact the risk/return profile of RE projects and, thus, their attractiveness. Market based incentives also have strong influence on investments by institutional investors. These measures support the need of investors for a highly reliable environment, best accompanied by a diminished risk exposure. Supportive regulatory measures such as codes and standards accelerate the diffusion process of RE technologies by further reducing technological and regulatory risk associated with investments in RE projects. Thus we recommend a supportive policy mix. The results of chapter 4 suggest the establishment of a reliable framework with a clear vision and long-term policy objectives regarding the sustainability transition.

When regulating clean technologies throughout industry development policy makers should keep all actors in mind as stated in chapter 5. Finance and innovation are usually separately regulated actors but as already found in chapter 2 largely interconnected. Thus, policy makers should regard immediate consequences and feedback mechanisms in their process. The rightly adjusted attention towards topics at the right point in life-cycle helps to support the growth trajectories of an industry. Thus, observing media is a possible way to recognize industry maturity and possible legitimacy of technologies.

6.5 Limitations and suggestions for future research

Even though this dissertation uses a multitude of approaches and data foundations a number of limitations to the results exist: The main focus lies on alternative investments in the clean technology and renewable energy industries. Thus the applicability to other industries may be limited due to peculiarity of this focus. Chapter 2 and 5 observe solely VC investments, chapter 4 only asset finance thus limiting transferability to other alternative asset classes or even different settings in financial markets. Similar, the focus on RE in chapter 4 and on solar energy and fuel cell technology in chapter 5 might limit general applicability. Furthermore regional settings, on the global level in chapter 2, comparing the USA and Germany in chapter 3, OECD country focus in chapter 4, and US industries in chapter 5 might impede comparability and transferability.

Methodological limitations regarding the approaches used occur as well in the studies. Quantitative content analysis has to face limitations inherent to the approach. Selection of analyzed data exposes the analysis to possible biases. In the case of chapter 2 and chapter 5, newspaper articles are the textual foundation. A broad selection and large quantities of data support the independence from researchers' expectations. Furthermore dictionary development can be influenced by the researcher and thus have to precede in a careful manner. A structured deductive approach, as used in both studies, prevents problems.(Elo & Kyngäs, 2007; Hsieh & Shannon, 2005). Similar the qualitative nature of chapter 3 leads to limitations with interview partner sampling, coding, and interpretation of results (K. Eisenhardt, 1989; Jick, 1979). Chapter 4 uses policy dummy variables and thus cannot differentiate between different policy characteristics (Bergek et al., 2013b; Jenner et al., 2013; Müller et al., 2011).

Based on the limitations of these studies, future research avenues open up. Not only could the results be tested in different industries or asset classes, regional settings and on different time frames, it would furthermore be advisable to confirm the findings in a more quantitative setting. In addition, research to test the complex interactions and interdependencies between finance, innovation, and, policy thus demand different methodological approaches. The emergence of investment categories and the role of finance in industry development offers various research opportunities. The transfer to other industries and detailed case studies would be interesting research. Comparing different evolutionary developments like cleantech to software or to biotech would be advisable to understand innovation accelerating conditions (Audretsch, 1995; Avnimelech & Teubal, 2006; O'Sullivan, 2005). The role of finance in innovation should get explored furthermore as well. The relationships between investors and their respective investors and the influence on innovation offers many opportunities to explore. How sustainability efforts of pension funds could possibly help to steer the sustainability transition is an interesting question for example (Bergek & Onufrey, 2013; Mary Jean Bürer & Wüstenhagen, 2008; Farla et al., 2012; Lovio et al., 2011).

Future studies could look at the influence of policies on the diffusion of RE in different settings. Extending this research regionally could help to look at differences in emerging and developing countries. Additionally interesting would the effects of policy on niche technologies be, which will get more important in the future. Wave and tide as well as off-shore wind energy might be interesting subjects. Furthermore, interaction effects between the different policy instruments are worthwhile investigating in a longitudinal research design to discover complementarities and synergies (Bergek et al., 2013a; Jenner et al., 2013; Lüthi & Wüstenhagen, 2012b; Müller et al., 2011).

This dissertation contributes to the research debate on how to accelerate green innovation and as well on the role of finance and policy in the clean technology innovation chain. Furthermore it adds some implications for investors, innovators, and policy makers. Hopefully, academic and industry stakeholders can utilize this work and build on the findings. As innovation in clean technologies is key to green growth, it is advisable to accelerate green innovation.

7 References

111th Congress of the United States of America. Dodd-Frank Wall Street Reform and Consumer Protection Act (2010). Retrieved from https://www.sec.gov/about/laws/wallstreetreform-cpa.pdf

Abernathy, W. J., & Utterback, J. M. (1978). Patterns of industrial innovation. *Technology Review*, *64*, 40–47.

Adams, P., Fontana, R., & Malerba, F. (2013). The magnitude of innovation by demand in a sectoral system: The role of industrial users in semiconductors. *Research Policy*, *42*(1), 1–14. https://doi.org/10.1016/j.respol.2012.05.011

Aghion, P., David, P. A., & Foray, D. (2009). Science, technology and innovation for economic growth: Linking policy research and practice in "STIG Systems." *Research Policy*, *38*(4), 681–693. https://doi.org/10.1016/j.respol.2009.01.016

Aguirre, M., & Ibikunle, G. (2014). Determinants of renewable energy growth: A global sample analysis. *Energy Policy*, *69*, 374–384. https://doi.org/10.1016/j.enpol.2014.02.036

Åhman, M. (2006). Government policy and the development of electric vehicles in Japan. *Energy Policy*, *34*(4), 433–443. https://doi.org/10.1016/j.enpol.2004.06.011

Aldrich, H. E., & Fiol, C. M. (1994). Fools Rush in? The Institutional Context of Industry Creation. *The Academy of Management Review*, *19*(4), 645. https://doi.org/10.2307/258740

Altenburg, T., & Pegels, A. (2012). Sustainability-oriented innovation systems – managing the green transformation. *Innovation and Development*, *2*(1), 5–22. https://doi.org/10.1080/2157930X.2012.664037

Angrist, J. D., & Pischke, J.-S. (2008). *Mostly Harmless Econometrics: An Empiricist's Companion*. Princeton University Press.

Arabatzis, G., & Myronidis, D. (2011). Contribution of SHP Stations to the development of an area and their social acceptance. *Renewable and Sustainable Energy Reviews*, *15*(8), 3909–3917. https://doi.org/10.1016/j.rser.2011.07.026

Arora, S., Romijn, H. A., & Caniëls, M. C. J. (2014). Governed by history: institutional analysis of a contested biofuel innovation system in Tanzania. *Industrial and Corporate Change*, *23*(2), 573–607. https://doi.org/10.1093/icc/dtt017

Audretsch, D. B. (1995). *Innovation and Industry Evolution*. Cambridge, MA: MIT Press.

Audretsch, D. B., & Feldman, M. P. (1996). R&D Spillovers and the Geography of Innovation and Production. *The American Economic Review*, *86*(3), 630–640.

Auerswald, P. E., & Branscomb, L. M. (2003). Valleys of Death and Darwinian Seas: Financing the Invention to Innovation Transition in the United States. *The Journal of Technology Transfer*, *28*(3–4), 227–239. https://doi.org/10.1023/A:1024980525678

Autio, E., Kenney, M., Mustar, P., Siegel, D., & Wright, M. (2014). Entrepreneurial innovation: The importance of context. *Research Policy*, *43*(7), 1097–1108. https://doi.org/10.1016/j.respol.2014.01.015

Avnimelech, G., Kenney, M., & Teubal, M. (2004). *Building Venture Capital Industries: Understanding the U.S. and Israeli Experiences* (BRIE Working Paper No. 160). Berkeley, CA: Berkeley Roundtable on the International Economy. Retrieved from http://escholarship.org/uc/item/9035c3vt

Avnimelech, G., & Teubal, M. (2006). Creating venture capital industries that co-evolve with high tech: Insights from an extended industry life cycle perspective of the Israeli experience. *Research Policy*, *35*(10), 1477–1498. https://doi.org/10.1016/j.respol.2006.09.017

Badcock, J., & Lenzen, M. (2010). Subsidies for electricity-generating technologies: A review. *Energy Policy*, *38*(9), 5038–5047. https://doi.org/10.1016/j.enpol.2010.04.031

Badino, J. H., Hu, C.-C., & Hung, C.-Y. (2006). Models of Taiwanese Venture Capital Activity and Paths for the Future. *Venture Capital*, *8*(3), 203–226.

Bank for International Settlements. (2010). *International regulatory framework for banks (Basel III)*. Retrieved from http://www.bis.org/bcbs/basel3.htm

Barradale, M. J. (2010). Impact of public policy uncertainty on renewable energy investment: Wind power and the production tax credit. *Energy Policy*, *38*(12), 7698–7709. https://doi.org/10.1016/j.enpol.2010.08.021

Barreto, L., & Kemp, R. (2007). Inclusion of technology diffusion in energy-systems models: some gaps and needs. *Journal of Cleaner Production*.

Becker, R., & Hellmann, T. (2003). *The Genesis of Venture Capital - Lessons from the German Experience* (CESifo Working Paper No. 883). CESifo.

Belke, A. H. (2013). *Impact of a low interest rate environment–Global liquidity spillovers and the search-for-yield* (ROME Discussion Paper Series). Bonn. Retrieved from http://papers.ssrn.com/sol3/papers.cfm?abstract_id=2309963

Berelson, B. (1952). *Content analysis in communication research.* New York, NY: Free Press.

Bergek, A., Jacobsson, S., Carlsson, B., Lindmark, S., & Rickne, A. (2008). Analyzing the Functional Dynamics of Technological Innovation Systems: A Scheme of

Analysis. *Research Policy*, *37*(3), 407–429. https://doi.org/10.1016/j.respol.2007.12.003

Bergek, A., Mignon, I., & Sundberg, G. (2013a). Who invests in renewable electricity production? Empirical evidence and suggestions for further research. *Energy Policy*, *56*, 568–581. https://doi.org/10.1016/j.enpol.2013.01.038

Bergek, A., Mignon, I., & Sundberg, G. (2013b). Who invests in renewable electricity production? Empirical evidence and suggestions for further research. *Energy Policy*, *56*, 568–581. https://doi.org/10.1016/j.enpol.2013.01.038

Bergek, A., & Onufrey, K. (2013). Is one path enough? Multiple paths and path interaction as an extension of path dependency theory. *Industrial and Corporate Change*. https://doi.org/10.1093/icc/dtt040

Berger, A., & Udell, G. (1998). The economics of small business finance: The roles of private equity and debt markets in the financial growth cycle. *Journal of Banking & Finance*, *22*(6–8), 613–673.

Bewley, T. (2002). Interviews as a valid empirical tool in economics. *The Journal of Socio-Economics*, *31*(4), 343–353. https://doi.org/10.1016/S1053-5357(02)00176-2

Bird, L. A., Bolinger, M., Gagliano, T., Wiser, R., Brown, M., & Parsons, B. (2005). Policies and market factors driving wind power development in the United States. *Energy Policy*, *33*(11), 1397–1407. https://doi.org/10.1016/j.enpol.2003.12.018

Block, J., & Sandner, P. (2009). What is the effect of the financial crisis on venture capital financing? Empirical evidence from US Internet start-ups. *Venture Capital*, *11*(4), 295–309. https://doi.org/10.1080/13691060903184803

BNEF. (2013). *Bloomberg New Energy Finance (BNEF)*. Bloomberg. Retrieved from http://www.bnef.com

Bocken, N. M. P. (2015). Sustainable venture capital – catalyst for sustainable start-up success? *Journal of Cleaner Production*, *108*(Part A), 647–658. https://doi.org/10.1016/j.jclepro.2015.05.079

Bolinger, M., Wiser, R., Milford, L., Stoddard, M., & Porter, K. (2001). States Emerge as Clean Energy Investors: A Review of State Support for Renewable Energy. *The Electricity Journal*, *14*(9), 82–95. https://doi.org/10.1016/S1040-6190(01)00246-9

Bolkesjø, T. F., Eltvig, P. T., & Nygaard, E. (2014). An Econometric Analysis of Support Scheme Effects on Renewable Energy Investments in Europe. *Energy Procedia*, *58*, 2–8. https://doi.org/10.1016/j.egypro.2014.10.401

Borrás, S., & Edquist, C. (2013). The choice of innovation policy instruments. *Technological Forecasting and Social Change*, *80*(8), 1513–1522. https://doi.org/10.1016/j.techfore.2013.03.002

Bottazzi, L., & Da Rin, M. (2002). Venture capital in Europe and the financing of innovative companies. *Economic Policy*, *17*(34), 229–270. https://doi.org/10.1111/1468-0327.00088

Bottazzi, L., & Rin, M. D. (2002). Venture capital in Europe and the financing of innovative companies. *Economic Policy*, *17*(34), 229–270. https://doi.org/10.1111/1468-0327.00088

Boykoff, M. T. (2008). The cultural politics of climate change discourse in UK tabloids. *Political Geography*, *27*(5), 549–569. https://doi.org/10.1016/j.polgeo.2008.05.002

Brossard, O., Lavigne, S., & Sakinç, M. E. (2013a). Ownership structures and R&D in Europe: the good institutional investors, the bad and ugly impatient shareholders. *Industrial and Corporate Change*, *22*(4), 1031–1068. https://doi.org/10.1093/icc/dtt018

Brossard, O., Lavigne, S., & Sakinç, M. E. (2013b). Ownership structures and R&D in Europe: the good institutional investors, the bad and ugly impatient shareholders. *Industrial and Corporate Change*, *22*(4), 1031–1068. https://doi.org/10.1093/icc/dtt018

Brown, M. A. (1990). The cost of commercializing energy inventions. *Research Policy*, *19*(2), 147–155. https://doi.org/10.1016/0048-7333(90)90044-7

Bürer, M. J. (2008). *Public Policy and Clean Energy Private Equity Investment.* University of St. Gallen, Graduate School of Business Administration, Economics, Law and Social Sciences (HSG), Zürich. Retrieved from http://www1.unisg.ch/www/edis.nsf/SysLkpByIdentifier/3421/$FILE/dis3421.pdf

Bürer, M. J., & Wüstenhagen, R. (2008). Cleantech Venture Investors and Energy Policy Risk: An Exploratory Analysis of Regulatory Risk Management Strategies. In R. Wüstenhagen, J. Hamschmidt, S. Sharma, & M. Starik (Eds.), *Sustainable Innovation and Entrepreneurship* (pp. 290–309). Cheltenham, UK: Edward Elgar Publishing.

Bürer, M. J., & Wüstenhagen, R. (2009). Which renewable energy policy is a venture capitalist's best friend? Empirical evidence from a survey of international cleantech investors. *Energy Policy*, *37*(12), 4997–5006. https://doi.org/10.1016/j.enpol.2009.06.071

Bürer, M. J., & Wüstenhagen, R. (2009). Which renewable energy policy is a venture capitalist's best friend? Empirical evidence from a survey of international cleantech investors. *Energy Policy*, *37*, 4997–5006. https://doi.org/10.1016/j.enpol.2009.06.071

Butler, L., & Neuhoff, K. (2008). Comparison of feed-in tariff, quota and auction mechanisms to support wind power development. *Renewable Energy*, *33*, 1854–1867.

Bygrave, W., Fast, N., Khoylian, R., Vincent, L., & William, Y. (1989). Early rates of return of 131 venture capital funds started 1978–1984. *Journal of Business Venturing*, *4*(2), 93–105. https://doi.org/10.1016/0883-9026(89)90024-4

Cameron, A. C., & Trivedi, P. K. (2009). *Microeconometrics using stata* (Vol. 5). Stata Press College Station, TX. Retrieved from http://stata.biz/news/statanews.23.4.pdf

Cansino, J. M., Pablo-Romero, M. del P., Román, R., & Yñiguez, R. (2010). Tax incentives to promote green electricity: An overview of EU-27 countries. *Energy Policy*, *38*(10), 6000–6008.

Caprotti, F. (2012). The cultural economy of cleantech: environmental discourse and the emergence of a new technology sector. *Transactions of the Institute of British Geographers*, *37*(3), 370–385. https://doi.org/10.1111/j.1475-5661.2011.00485.x

Cárdenas-Rodríguez, M., Johnstone, N., Haščič, I., Silva, J., & Ferey, A. (2013). Inducing private finance for renewable energy projects: Evidence from micro-data. *OECD Environment Working Papers*.

Carley, S. (2009). State renewable energy electricity policies: An empirical evaluation of effectiveness. *Energy Policy*, *37*(8), 3071–3081. https://doi.org/10.1016/j.enpol.2009.03.062

Chassot, S., Hampl, N., & Wüstenhagen, R. (2014). When energy policy meets free-market capitalists: The moderating influence of worldviews on risk perception and renewable energy investment decisions. *Energy Research & Social Science*, *3*, 143–151. https://doi.org/10.1016/j.erss.2014.07.013

Cheng, L. (2009). Are VCs Lemmings? Retrieved from http://larrycheng.com/2009/10/28/are-vcs-lemmings/

Chu, P., & Hisrich, R. D. (2001). Venture capital in an economy in transition. *Venture Capital*, *3*(2), 169–182. https://doi.org/10.1080/13691060110042772

Coenen, L., Benneworth, P., & Truffer, B. (2012). Toward a spatial perspective on sustainability transitions. *Research Policy*, *41*(6), 968–979. https://doi.org/10.1016/j.respol.2012.02.014

Comin, D., & Nanda, R. (2014). *Financial Development and Technology Diffusion* (Harvard Business School Working Paper No. No. 15-036). Boston: Harvard Business School. Retrieved from http://papers.ssrn.com/abstract=2520551

Cooke, P., Gomez Uranga, M., & Etxebarria, G. (1997). Regional Innovation Systems: Institutional and Organisational Dimensions. *Research Policy*, *26*(4), 475–491.

Cooke, P., & Morgan, K. (1994). The Creative Milieu: A Regional Perspective on Innovation. In M. Dodgson & R. Rothwell (Eds.), *The Handbook of Industrial Innovation* (pp. 25–32). Cheltenham, UK: Edward Elgar Publishing.

Corbin, J., & Strauss, A. (1994). Grounded Theory Methodology. In N. K. Denzin & Y. S. Lincoln (Eds.), *Handbook of Qualitative Research* (pp. 273–285). Thousand Oaks: Sage Publications.

Couture, T., & Gagnon, Y. (2010). An analysis of feed-in tariff remuneration models: Implications for renewable energy investment. *Energy Policy*, *38*(2), 955–965. https://doi.org/10.1016/j.enpol.2009.10.047

Creswell, J. W. (2003). *Research design: qualitative, quantitative, and mixed method approaches*. Thousand Oaks, Calif.: Sage Publications.

Criscuolo, C., & Menon, C. (2015). Environmental policies and risk finance in the green sector: Cross-country evidence. *Energy Policy*, *83*, 38–56. https://doi.org/10.1016/j.enpol.2015.03.023

Cumming, D. J., Henriques, I., & Sadorsky, P. (2013). *"Cleantech" Venture Capital Around the World* (SSRN Scholarly Paper No. ID 2323589). Rochester, NY: Social Science Research Network. Retrieved from http://papers.ssrn.com/abstract=2323589

Da Rin, M., Hellmann, T. F., & Puri, M. (2011). *A survey of venture capital research* (Working Paper No. 17523). National Bureau of Economic Research. Retrieved from http://www.nber.org/papers/w17523

Da Rin, M., Nicodano, G., & Sembenelli, A. (2006a). Public policy and the creation of active venture capital markets. *Journal of Public Economics*, *90*(8–9), 1699–1723. https://doi.org/10.1016/j.jpubeco.2005.09.013

Da Rin, M., Nicodano, G., & Sembenelli, A. (2006b). Public policy and the creation of active venture capital markets. *Journal of Public Economics*, *90*(8–9), 1699–1723. https://doi.org/10.1016/j.jpubeco.2005.09.013

De Jager, D., Klessmann, C., Stricker, E., Winkel, T., de Visser, E., Koper, M., Bouillé, A. (2011). *Financing Renewable Energy in the European Energy Market* (No. PECPNL084659) (p. 264). Ecofys, Fraunhofer ISI, TU Vienna EEG, Ernst & Young.

De Jager, D., Rathmann, M., Klessmann, C., Coenraads, R., Colamonico, C., & Buttazzoni, M. (2008). Policy instrument design to reduce financing costs in renewable energy technology projects. *Ecofys, by Order of the IEA Implementing Agreement on Renewable Energy Technology Deployment (RETD), Utrecht, Ther Netherlands*. Retrieved from http://www.researchgate.net/publication/258261301_Policy_instrument_design_to_reduce_financing_costs_in_renewable_energy_technology_projects/file/50463528c9f09b45ae.pdf

Déjean, F., Gond, J.-P., & Leca, B. (2004). Measuring the Unmeasured: An Institutional Entrepreneur Strategy in an Emerging Industry. *Human Relations*, *57*(6), 741–764. https://doi.org/10.1177/0018726704044954

del Río, P., & Bleda, M. (2012). Comparing the innovation effects of support schemes for renewable electricity technologies: A function of innovation approach. *Energy Policy*, *50*, 272–282. https://doi.org/10.1016/j.enpol.2012.07.014

Delmas, M. A., & Montes-Sancho, M. J. (2011). U.S. state policies for renewable energy: Context and effectiveness. *Energy Policy*, *39*(5), 2273–2288. https://doi.org/10.1016/j.enpol.2011.01.034

Destin, F. (2012). The Great European Venture Capital Crisis. Retrieved May 27, 2015, from http://freddestin.com/2012/05/the-great-european-venture-capital-crisis.html

Diefendorf, S. (2000). Venture capital & the environmental industry. *Corporate Environmental Strategy*, *7*(4), 388–399. https://doi.org/10.1016/S1066-7938(00)90010-1

Dimov, D., Holan, P. M. de, & Milanov, H. (2012). Learning patterns in venture capital investing in new industries. *Industrial and Corporate Change*, *21*(6), 1389–1426. https://doi.org/10.1093/icc/dts010

Dinica, V. (2006). Support systems for the diffusion of renewable energy technologies—an investor perspective. *Energy Policy*, *34*(4), 461–480. https://doi.org/10.1016/j.enpol.2004.06.014

Dodgson, M., Mathews, J., Kastelle, T., & Hu, M.-C. (2008). The evolving nature of Taiwan's national innovation system: The case of biotechnology innovation networks. *Research Policy*, *37*(3), 430–445. https://doi.org/10.1016/j.respol.2007.12.005

Dosi, G. (1990). Finance, innovation and industrial change. *Journal of Economic Behavior & Organization*, *13*(3), 299–319. https://doi.org/10.1016/0167-2681(90)90003-V

Economist. (2012, April 9). Venturecrats. Retrieved July 13, 2014, from http://www.economist.com/blogs/schumpeter/2012/04/european-venture-capital

Edquist, C. (2005). Systems of innovation. In J. Fagerberg, D. C. Mowery, & R. R. Nelson (Eds.), *The Oxford Handbook of Innovation* (pp. 181–208). Oxford; New York: Oxford University Press, U.S.A.

Edquist, C. (2011). Design of Innovation Policy through Diagnostic Analysis: Identification of Systemic Problems (or Failures). *Industrial and Corporate Change*, *20*(6), 1725–1753.

Eichhammer, W., Ragwitz, M., & Schlomann, B. (2013). Introduction to the Special Issue: Financing Instruments to Promote Energy Efficiency and Renewables in

Times of Tight Public Budgets. *Energy & Environment*, *24*(1), 1–26. https://doi.org/10.1260/0958-305X.24.1-2.1

Eisenhardt, K. (1989). Building Theories from Case Study Research. *Academy of Management Review*, *14*(4), 532–550.

Eisenhardt, K. M. (1989). Building Theories from Case Study Research. *The Academy of Management Review*, *14*(4), 532–550.

Elo, S., & Kyngäs, H. (2007). The qualitative content analysis process. *Journal of Advanced Nursing*, *62*(1), 107–115. https://doi.org/10.1111/j.1365-2648.2007.04569.x

Ettenhuber, C. (2013). *Financing corporate growth in the renewable energy industry*. Frankfurt am Main: PL Acad. Research.

European Commission. (2014). Solvency. Retrieved July 13, 2014, from http://ec.europa.eu/internal_market/insurance/solvency/index_en.htm

Fagerberg, J., & Verspagen, B. (2002). Technology-gaps, innovation-diffusion and transformation: an evolutionary interpretation. *Research Policy*, *31*(8), 1291–1304.

Farla, J., Markard, J., Raven, R., & Coenen, L. (2012). Sustainability transitions in the making: A closer look at actors, strategies and resources. *Technological Forecasting and Social Change*, *79*(6), 991–998. https://doi.org/10.1016/j.techfore.2012.02.001

Feldman, M. P. (1993). An Examination of the Geography of Innovation. *Industrial and Corporate Change*, *2*(3), 451–470. https://doi.org/10.1093/icc/2.3.451

Filippetti, A., & Archibugi, D. (2011). Innovation in times of crisis: National Systems of Innovation, structure, and demand. *Research Policy*, *40*(2), 179–192. https://doi.org/10.1016/j.respol.2010.09.001

Fischlein, M., Larson, J., Hall, D. M., Chaudhry, R., Rai Peterson, T., Stephens, J. C., & Wilson, E. J. (2010). Policy stakeholders and deployment of wind power in the sub-national context: A comparison of four U.S. states. *Energy Policy*, *38*(8), 4429–4439. https://doi.org/10.1016/j.enpol.2010.03.073

Flanagan, K., Uyarra, E., & Laranja, M. (2011a). Reconceptualising the "policy mix" for innovation. *Research Policy*, *40*(5), 702–713. https://doi.org/10.1016/j.respol.2011.02.005

Flanagan, K., Uyarra, E., & Laranja, M. (2011b). Reconceptualising the "policy mix" for innovation. *Research Policy*, *40*(5), 702–713. https://doi.org/10.1016/j.respol.2011.02.005

Florida, R., & Kenney, M. (1988a). Venture capital and high technology entrepreneurship. *Journal of Business Venturing*, *3*(4), 301–319. https://doi.org/10.1016/0883-9026(88)90011-0

Florida, R., & Kenney, M. (1988b). Venture capital-financed innovation and technological change in the USA. *Research Policy, 17*(3), 119–137.

Foxon, T. J., & Pearson, P. (2008a). Overcoming barriers to innovation and diffusion of cleaner technologies: some features of a sustainable innovation policy regime. *Journal of Cleaner Production, 16*(1), 148–161. https://doi.org/10.1016/j.jclepro.2007.10.011

Foxon, T. J., & Pearson, P. G. (2008b). Overcoming barriers to innovation and diffusion of cleaner technologies: some features of a sustainable innovation policy regime. *Journal of Cleaner Production, 16*(1, Supplement 1), S148–S161. https://doi.org/10.1016/j.jclepro.2007.10.011

Foxon, T. J., & Pearson, P. J. G. (2007). Towards improved policy processes for promoting innovation in renewable electricity technologies in the UK. *Energy Policy, 35*(3), 1539–1550. https://doi.org/10.1016/j.enpol.2006.04.009

Francis, J. J., Johnston, M., Robertson, C., Glidewell, L., Entwistle, V., Eccles, M. P., & Grimshaw, J. M. (2010). What is an adequate sample size? Operationalising data saturation for theory-based interview studies. *Psychology & Health, 25*(10), 1229–1245. https://doi.org/10.1080/08870440903194015

Fraser-Sampson, G. (2011). *Private Equity as an Asset Class*. John Wiley & Sons.

Fraunhofer ISE. (2014). *Photovoltaics Report*. Retrieved from http://www.ise.fraunhofer.de/de/downloads/pdf-files/aktuelles/photovoltaics-report-in-englischer-sprache.pdf

Friebe, C. A., Flotow, P. von, & Täube, F. A. (2013). Exploring the link between products and services in low-income markets—Evidence from solar home systems. *Energy Policy, 52*, 760–769. https://doi.org/10.1016/j.enpol.2012.10.038

Friebe, C. A., von Flotow, P., & Täube, F. A. (2014). Exploring technology diffusion in emerging markets – the role of public policy for wind energy. *Energy Policy, 70*, 217–226. https://doi.org/10.1016/j.enpol.2014.03.016

Garud, R., & Karnøe, P. (2003). Bricolage versus breakthrough: distributed and embedded agency in technology entrepreneurship. *Research Policy, 32*(2), 277–300. https://doi.org/10.1016/S0048-7333(02)00100-2

Geels, F. W. (2014). Reconceptualising the co-evolution of firms-in-industries and their environments: Developing an inter-disciplinary Triple Embeddedness Framework. *Research Policy, 43*(2), 261–277. https://doi.org/10.1016/j.respol.2013.10.006

Ghosh, S., & Nanda, R. (2010). *Venture capital investment in the clean energy sector*. Harvard Business School.

Glaser, B. G., & Strauss, A. L. (1967). *The Discovery of Grounded Theory: Strategies for Qualitative Research*. New Brunswick, NJ: Transaction Publishers.

Godoe, H., & Nygaard, S. (2006). System failure, innovation policy and patents: Fuel cells and related hydrogen technology in Norway 1990-2002. *Energy Policy, 34*(13), 1697–1708. https://doi.org/10.1016/j.enpol.2004.12.016

Gompers, P., & Lerner, J. (2001). The Venture Capital Revolution. *The Journal of Economic Perspectives, 15*(2), 145–168.

Graham, A. (2005). Pressman/Wildavsky and Bardach: Implementation in the public sector, past, present and future. *Canadian Public Administration, 48*(2), 268–273. https://doi.org/10.1111/j.1754-7121.2005.tb02191.x

Greentech Media. (2014). DOE: The Clean Energy Loan Program Is Already Making a Profit for Taxpayers. Retrieved from http://www.greentechmedia.com/articles/read/The-Clean-Energy-Loan-Program-Is-Already-Making-Money-for-Taxpayers.

Greer, R. J. (1997). What is an Asset Class, Anyway? *The Journal of Portfolio Management, 23*(2), 86–91. https://doi.org/10.3905/jpm.23.2.86

Grilli, L., & Murtinu, S. (2014). New technology-based firms in Europe: market penetration, public venture capital, and timing of investment. *Industrial and Corporate Change*, dtu025. https://doi.org/10.1093/icc/dtu025

Hair, J. (2010). *Multivariate data analysis : a global perspective.* (7th ed. /). Upper Saddle River N.J., London: Pearson Education.

Haislip, A. (2010). *Essentials of Venture Capital*. John Wiley & Sons.

Haley, U. C., & Schuler, D. A. (2011). Government Policy and Firm Strategy in the Solar Photovoltaic Industry. *California Management Review, 54*(1), 17–38.

Haley, U. C. V., & Schuler, D. A. (2011). Government Policy and Firm Strategy in the Solar Photovoltaic Industry. *California Management Review, 54*(1), 17–38. https://doi.org/10.1525/cmr.2011.54.1.17

Hall, J., & Kerr, R. (2003). Innovation dynamics and environmental technologies: the emergence of fuel cell technology. *Journal of Cleaner Production, 11*(4), 459–471. https://doi.org/10.1016/S0959-6526(02)00067-7

Hargadon, A. B., & Kenney, M. (2012). Misguided Policy? Following Venture Capital into Clean Technology. *California Management Review, 54*(2), 118–139. https://doi.org/10.1525/cmr.2012.54.2.118

Harmelink, M., Voogt, M., & Cremer, C. (2006). Analysing the effectiveness of renewable energy supporting policies in the European Union. *Energy Policy, 34*(3), 343–351. https://doi.org/10.1016/j.enpol.2004.08.031

Heck, S., Rogers, M., & Carroll, P. (2014). *Resource Revolution: How to Capture the Biggest Business Opportunity in a Century*. Amazon Publishing.

Hekkert, M. P., Suurs, R. A. A., Negro, S. O., Kuhlmann, S., & Smits, R. E. H. M. (2007). Functions of Innovation Systems: A New Approach for Analysing

Technological Change. *Technological Forecasting and Social Change*, *74*(4), 413–432. https://doi.org/10.1016/j.techfore.2006.03.002

Hellman, H. L., & van den Hoed, R. (2007). Characterising fuel cell technology: Challenges of the commercialisation process. *International Journal of Hydrogen Energy*, *32*, 35–315.

Helm, D. (2002). Energy policy: security of supply, sustainability and competition. *Energy Policy*, *30*(3), 173–184.

Hendry, C., & Harborne, P. (2011). Changing the view of wind power development: More than "bricolage." *Research Policy*, *40*(5), 778–789. https://doi.org/10.1016/j.respol.2011.03.001

Henriot, A. (2013). Financing investment in the European electricity transmission network: Consequences on long-term sustainability of the TSOs financial structure. *Energy Policy*, *62*, 821–829. https://doi.org/10.1016/j.enpol.2013.07.011

Hess, D. J. (2014). Sustainability transitions: A political coalition perspective. *Research Policy*, *43*(2), 278–283. https://doi.org/10.1016/j.respol.2013.10.008

Hirsch-Kreinsen, H. (2011). Financial Market and Technological Innovation. *Industry & Innovation*, *18*(4), 351–368. https://doi.org/10.1080/13662716.2011.573954

Hockerts, K., & Wüstenhagen, R. (2010a). Greening Goliaths versus emerging Davids — Theorizing about the Role of Incumbents and New Entrants in Sustainable Entrepreneurship. *Journal of Business Venturing*, *25*(5), 481–492. https://doi.org/10.1016/j.jbusvent.2009.07.005

Hockerts, K., & Wüstenhagen, R. (2010b). Greening Goliaths versus emerging Davids — Theorizing about the role of incumbents and new entrants in sustainable entrepreneurship. *Journal of Business Venturing*, *25*(5), 481–492. https://doi.org/10.1016/j.jbusvent.2009.07.005

Hoffman, A. J. (1999). Institutional Evolution and Change: Environmentalism and the U.S. Chemical Industry. *Academy of Management Journal*, *42*(4), 351–371. https://doi.org/10.2307/257008

Hoppmann, J. (2014). The Role of Deployment Policies in Fostering Innovation for Clean Energy Technologies Insights From the Solar Photovoltaic Industry. *Business & Society*, 0007650314558042. https://doi.org/10.1177/0007650314558042

Hoppmann, J., Huenteler, J., & Girod, B. (2014). Compulsive policy-making—The evolution of the German feed-in tariff system for solar photovoltaic power. *Research Policy*, *43*(8), 1422–1441. https://doi.org/10.1016/j.respol.2014.01.014

Hoppmann, J., Peters, M., Schneider, M., & Hoffmann, V. H. (2013). The two faces of market support—How deployment policies affect technological exploration and exploitation in the solar photovoltaic industry. *Research Policy*, *42*(4), 989–1003. https://doi.org/10.1016/j.respol.2013.01.002

Howell, S. T. (2014). *Financing Constraints as Barriers to Innovation: Evidence from R&D Grants to Energy Startups*. Cambridge: Harvard University. Retrieved from http://scholar.harvard.edu/files/showell/files/howell_innovation_finance_jmp_oct26.pdf

Hsieh, H. F., & Shannon, S. E. (2005). Three Approaches to Qualitative Content Analysis. *Qualitative Health Research*, *15*(9), 1277–1288. https://doi.org/10.1177/1049732305276687

Huberman, M., & Miles, M. B. (2002). *The qualitative researcher's companion*. London: Sage Publications.

IEA. (2013). *Tracking Clean Energy Progress 2013*. Paris: IEA. Retrieved from http://www.iea.org/etp/tracking/

IEA. (2014). IEA FAQ Renewable Energy. Retrieved from http://www.iea.org/aboutus/faqs/renewableenergy/

IPCC. (2014). *Climate Change 2014: Mitigation of climate change - IPCC Working Group III Contribution to AR5* (p. 33). Berlin: Int.

IRENA. (2016). Renewable Capacity Statistics 2016. Retrieved from http://www.irena.org/DocumentDownloads/Publications/IRENA_RE_Capacity_Statistics_2016.pdf

Iyer, G., Hultman, N., Eom, J., McJeon, H., Patel, P., & Clarke, L. (2015). Diffusion of low-carbon technologies and the feasibility of long-term climate targets. *Technological Forecasting and Social Change*, *90*, 103–118. https://doi.org/10.1016/j.techfore.2013.08.025

Jacobsson, S., & Bergek, A. (2004). Transforming the energy sector: the evolution of technological systems in renewable energy technology. *Industrial and Corporate Change*, *13*(5), 815–849. https://doi.org/10.1093/icc/dth032

Jacobsson, S., & Bergek, A. (2011). Innovation system analyses and sustainability transitions: Contributions and suggestions for research. *Environmental Innovation and Societal Transitions*, *1*(1), 41–57. https://doi.org/10.1016/j.eist.2011.04.006

Jacobsson, S., Bergek, A., Finon, D., Lauber, V., Mitchell, C., Toke, D., & Verbruggen, A. (2009). EU renewable energy support policy: Faith or facts? *Energy Policy*, *37*(6), 2143–2146. https://doi.org/10.1016/j.enpol.2009.02.043

Jefferson, M. (2008). Accelerating the transition to sustainable energy systems. *Energy Policy*, *36*(11), 4116–4125. https://doi.org/10.1016/j.enpol.2008.06.020

Jeng, L. A., & Wells, P. C. (2000). The determinants of venture capital funding: evidence across countries. *Journal of Corporate Finance*, *6*(3), 241–289. https://doi.org/10.1016/S0929-1199(00)00003-1

Jenner, S., Groba, F., & Indvik, J. (2013). Assessing the strength and effectiveness of renewable electricity feed-in tariffs in European Union countries. *Energy Policy*, *52*, 385–401. https://doi.org/10.1016/j.enpol.2012.09.046

Jensen, S. G., & Skytte, K. (2002). Interactions between the power and green certificate markets. *Energy Policy*, *30*(5), 425–435. https://doi.org/10.1016/S0301-4215(01)00111-2

Jick, T. D. (1979). Mixing qualitative and quantitative methods: Triangulation in action. *Administrative Science Quarterly*, 602–611.

Johnson, A. (2001). Functions in innovation system approaches. In *Dannish Research Unit for Industrial Dynamics (DRUID)*. Retrieved from http://www.druid.dk/conferences/nw/paper1/a_johnson.pdf

Johnstone, N., Haščič, I., & Popp, D. (2010a). Renewable Energy Policies and Technological Innovation: Evidence Based on Patent Counts. *Environmental and Resource Economics*, *45*(1), 133–155. https://doi.org/10.1007/s10640-009-9309-1

Johnstone, N., Haščič, I., & Popp, D. (2010b). Renewable Energy Policies and Technological Innovation: Evidence Based on Patent Counts. *Environmental and Resource Economics*, *45*(1), 133–155. https://doi.org/10.1007/s10640-009-9309-1

Kaminker, C., & Stewart, F. (2012). *The role of institutional investors in financing clean energy*. OECD Publishing. Retrieved from http://www.oecd.org/finance/private-pensions/WP_23_TheRoleOfInstitutionalInvestorsInFinancingCleanEnergy.pdf

Karaomerlioglu, D. C., & Jacobsson, S. (2000). The Swedish venture capital industry: an infant, adolescent or grown-up? *Venture Capital*, *2*(1), 61–88. https://doi.org/10.1080/136910600295819

Kennedy, M. T. (2005). Behind the one-way mirror: Refraction in the construction of product market categories. *Poetics*, *33*(3–4), 201–226. https://doi.org/10.1016/j.poetic.2005.09.012

Kenney, M. (2011a). How venture capital became a component of the US National System of Innovation. *Industrial and Corporate Change*, *20*(6), 1677–1723. https://doi.org/10.1093/icc/dtr061

Kenney, M. (2011b). Venture Capital Investment in the Greentech Industries: A Provocative Essay. In R. Wüstenhagen & R. Wuebker (Eds.), *The Handbook of Research on Energy Entrepreneurship* (p. 214). Cheltenham, UK: Edward Elgar Publishing.

Kenney, M., & Hargadon, A. (2012). Misguided Policy? *California Management Review*, *54*(2), 118–139. https://doi.org/10.1525/cmr.2012.54.2.118

Khaire, M., & Wadhwani, R. D. (2010). Changing landscapes: The construction of meaning and value in a new market category—Modern Indian art. *Academy of Management Journal*, *53*(6), 1281–1304.

Klepper, S. (1996). Entry, Exit, Growth, and Innovation over the Product Life Cycle. *The American Economic Review*, *86*(3), 562–583.

Klepper, S. (1997). Industry life cycles. *Industrial and Corporate Change*, *6*(1), 145–182.

Knowles, V. (2013). *European Cleantech Fundraising 2013-14: Investors have their own chasm to cross*. Retrieved from http://www.georgieffcapital.com/docs/uploads/0854008001366391730.pdf

Kortum, S., & Lerner, J. (2000a). Assessing the Contribution of Venture Capital to Innovation. *RAND Journal of Economics*, *31*(4), 674–692.

Kortum, S., & Lerner, J. (2000b). Assessing the Contribution of Venture Capital to Innovation. *The RAND Journal of Economics*, *31*(4), 674–692. https://doi.org/10.2307/2696354

Krippendorff, K. (2012). *Content analysis: An introduction to its methodology*. Sage.

Lacy, S. (2008). *Once You're Lucky, Twice You're Good: The Rebirth of Silicon Valley and the Rise of Web 2.0*. Penguin.

Leete, S., Xu, J., & Wheeler, D. (2013). Investment barriers and incentives for marine renewable energy in the UK: An analysis of investor preferences. *Energy Policy*, *60*, 866–875. https://doi.org/10.1016/j.enpol.2013.05.011

Lerner, J. (2002). Boom and Bust in the Venture Capital Industry and the Impact on Innovation. *Federal Reserve Bank of Atlanta Economic Review*, *87*(4), 25–39.

Lerner, J. (2009). *Boulevard of Broken Dreams: Why Public Efforts to Boost Entrepreneurship and Venture Capital Have Failed—and What to Do About It*. Princeton: Princeton University Press.

Lerner, J., Sorensen, M., & Strömberg, P. (2011). Private Equity and Long-Run Investment: The Case of Innovation. *The Journal of Finance*, *66*(2), 445–477. https://doi.org/10.1111/j.1540-6261.2010.01639.x

Lerner, J., & Tåg, J. (2013a). Institutions and venture capital. *Industrial and Corporate Change*, *22*(1), 153–182. https://doi.org/10.1093/icc/dts050

Lerner, J., & Tåg, J. (2013b). Institutions and venture capital. *Industrial and Corporate Change*, *22*(1), 153–182. https://doi.org/10.1093/icc/dts050

Lesser, J., & Su, X. (2008). Design of an economically efficient feed-in tariff structure for renewable energy development. *Energy Policy*, *36*, 981–990.

Levine, R. (2005). Finance and Growth: Theory and Evidence. In P. A. and S. N. Durlauf (Ed.), *Handbook of Economic Growth* (Vol. 1, Part A, pp. 865–934). Elsevier. Retrieved from http://www.sciencedirect.com/science/article/pii/S1574068405010129

Lovio, R., Mickwitz, P., & Heiskanen, E. (2011). Path Dependence, Path Creation and Creative Destruction in the Evolution of Energy Systems. In R. Wüstenhagen & R. Wuebker (Eds.), *The Handbook of Research on Energy Entrepreneurship* (p. 274). Cheltenham, UK: Edward Elgar Publishing.

Lundvall, B.-Å. (1992). Introduction. In B.-Å. Lundvall (Ed.), *National Systems of Innovation - toward a Theory of Innovation and Interactive Learning* (pp. 1–19). London: Pinter Publishers.

Lüthi, S., & Prässler, T. (2011). Analyzing policy support instruments and regulatory risk factors for wind energy deployment—A developers' perspective. *Energy Policy*, *39*(9), 4876–4892. https://doi.org/10.1016/j.enpol.2011.06.029

Lüthi, S., & Wüstenhagen, R. (2012a). The price of policy risk — Empirical insights from choice experiments with European photovoltaic project developers. *Energy Economics*, *34*(4), 1001–1011. https://doi.org/10.1016/j.eneco.2011.08.007

Lüthi, S., & Wüstenhagen, R. (2012b). The price of policy risk — Empirical insights from choice experiments with European photovoltaic project developers. *Energy Economics*, *34*(4), 1001–1011. https://doi.org/10.1016/j.eneco.2011.08.007

Magro, E., & Wilson, J. R. (2013). Complex innovation policy systems: Towards an evaluation mix. *Research Policy*, *42*(9), 1647–1656. https://doi.org/10.1016/j.respol.2013.06.005

Malerba, F. (2002). Sectoral systems of innovation and production. *Research Policy*, *31*(2), 247–264.

Malerba, F., Nelson, R. R., Orsenigo, L., & Winter, S. (1999). "History-friendly" models of industry evolution: the computer industry. *Industrial and Corporate Change*, *8*(1), 3–40. https://doi.org/10.1093/icc/8.1.3

Malerba, F., & Orsenigo, L. (1996). The Dynamics and Evolution of Industries. *Industrial and Corporate Change*, *5*(1), 51–87. https://doi.org/10.1093/icc/5.1.51

Marcus, A., Aragon-Correa, J. A., & Pinkse, J. (2011). Firms, regulatory uncertainty, and the natural environment. *California Management Review*, *54*(1), 5–16.

Marcus, A., Ellis, S., Malen, J., Drori, I., & Sened, I. (2011). Path Dependence and Creation in Venture Capital Investment. In A. Marcus, P. Shrivastava, S. Sharma, & S. Pogutz (Eds.), *Cross-Sector Leadership for the Green Economy*. New York, NY: Palgrave Macmillan.

Marcus, A., Malen, J., & Ellis, S. (2013). The Promise and Pitfalls of Venture Capital as an Asset Class for Clean Energy Investment Research Questions for Organization and Natural Environment Scholars. *Organization & Environment, 26*(1), 31–60. https://doi.org/10.1177/1086026612474956

Markard, J., Raven, R., & Truffer, B. (2012). Sustainability transitions: An emerging field of research and its prospects. *Research Policy, 41*(6), 955–967. https://doi.org/10.1016/j.respol.2012.02.013

Marques, A. C., & Fuinhas, J. A. (2011). Do energy efficiency measures promote the use of renewable sources? *Environmental Science & Policy, 14*(4), 471–481. https://doi.org/10.1016/j.envsci.2011.02.001

Marques, A. C., & Fuinhas, J. A. (2012a). Are public policies towards renewables successful? Evidence from European countries. *Renewable Energy, 44*, 109–118. https://doi.org/10.1016/j.renene.2012.01.007

Marques, A. C., & Fuinhas, J. A. (2012b). Is renewable energy effective in promoting growth? *Energy Policy, 46*, 434–442. https://doi.org/10.1016/j.enpol.2012.04.006

Marques, A. C., Fuinhas, J. A., & Pires Manso, J. R. (2010). Motivations driving renewable energy in European countries: A panel data approach. *Energy Policy, 38*(11), 6877–6885. https://doi.org/10.1016/j.enpol.2010.07.003

Marshall, A. (1920). *Principles of economics*. London: Macmillan and Co., Ltd.

Masini, A., & Menichetti, E. (2012). The impact of behavioural factors in the renewable energy investment decision making process: Conceptual framework and empirical findings. *Energy Policy, 40*, 28–38. https://doi.org/10.1016/j.enpol.2010.06.062

Mason, C. (2009). Venture Capital in Crisis? Editorial. *Venture Capital, 11*(4), 279–285.

Mathews, J. A., Kidney, S., Mallon, K., & Hughes, M. (2010a). Mobilizing private finance to drive an energy industrial revolution. *Energy Policy, 38*(7), 3263–3265. https://doi.org/10.1016/j.enpol.2010.02.030

Mathews, J. A., Kidney, S., Mallon, K., & Hughes, M. (2010b). Mobilizing private finance to drive an energy industrial revolution. *Energy Policy, 38*, 3263–3265.

Mazzucato, M. (2000). Firm Size, Innovation, and Market Share Instability: the Role of Negative Feedback and Idiosyncratic Events. *Advances in Complex Systems, 03*(01n04), 417–431. https://doi.org/10.1142/S0219525900000297

Mazzucato, M. (2013a). Financing Innovation: Creative Destruction vs. Destructive Creation. *Industrial and Corporate Change, 22*(4), 851–867.

Mazzucato, M. (2013b). *The entrepreneurial state: Debunking public vs. private sector myths*. London: Anthem Press.

Mazzucato, M., & Perez, C. (2014). *Innovation as Growth Policy: the challenge for Europe* (SPRU Working Paper Series No. SWPS 2014-13). SPRU.

McCrone, A. (2015). *Global Trends in Renewable Energy Investment 2015*. Frankfurt am Main: Frankfurt School-UNEP Centre/BNEF.

McGrath, R. N. (1998). Technological discontinuities and media patterns: assessing electric vehicle batteries. *Technovation, 18*(11), 677–687. https://doi.org/10.1016/S0166-4972(98)00061-3

Menanteau, P., Finon, D., & Lamy, M.-L. (2003). Prices versus quantities: choosing policies for promoting the development of renewable energy. *Energy Policy, 31*(8), 799–812.

Menz, F. C., & Vachon, S. (2006). The effectiveness of different policy regimes for promoting wind power: Experiences from the states. *Energy Policy, 34*(14), 1786–1796. https://doi.org/10.1016/j.enpol.2004.12.018

Migendt, M., Täube, F. A., Gilbert, B. A., & von Flotow, V. (2014). *Emergence of Cleantech as an Investment Category - Public Discourse and Venture Capital Investment* (SSRN Scholarly Paper No. ID 2388656). Rochester, NY: Social Science Research Network. Retrieved from http://papers.ssrn.com/abstract=2388656

Miller, D., & Garnsey, E. (2000). Entrepreneurs and technology diffusion: How diffusion research can benefit from a greater understanding of entrepreneurship. *Technology in Society, 22*(4), 445–465.

Mina, A., Lahr, H., & Hughes, A. (2013). The demand and supply of external finance for innovative firms. *Industrial and Corporate Change, 22*(4), 869–901. https://doi.org/10.1093/icc/dtt020

Mingo, S., & Khanna, T. (2014). Industrial policy and the creation of new industries: evidence from Brazil's bioethanol industry. *Industrial and Corporate Change, 23*(5), 1229–1260. https://doi.org/10.1093/icc/dtt039

Mints, P. (2006). PV–the story so far: How is the PV industry progressing in its bid to be considered mainstream? *Refocus, 7*(6), 32–36.

Mitchell, C., Bauknecht, D., & Connor, P. M. (2006). Effectiveness through risk reduction: a comparison of the renewable obligation in England and Wales and the feed-in system in Germany. *Energy Policy, 34*(3), 297–305. https://doi.org/10.1016/j.enpol.2004.08.004

Moran-Ellis, J., Alexander, V. D., Cronin, A., Dickinson, M., Fielding, J., Sleney, J., & Thomas, H. (2006). Triangulation and integration: processes, claims and implications. *Qualitative Research, 6*(1), 45–59. https://doi.org/10.1177/1468794106058870

Mowery, D. C., Nelson, R. R., & Martin, B. R. (2010a). Technology Policy and Global Warming: Why New Policy Models Are Needed (or Why Putting New Wine in Old Bottles Won't Work). *Research Policy*, *39*(8), 1011–1023.

Mowery, D. C., Nelson, R. R., & Martin, B. R. (2010b). Technology policy and global warming: Why new policy models are needed (or why putting new wine in old bottles won't work). *Research Policy*, *39*, 1011–1023.

Müller, S., Brown, A., & Ölz, S. (2011). Renewable energy: policy considerations for deploying renewables. *International Energy Agency*.

Nanda, R., Younge, K., & Fleming, L. (2014). Innovation and Entrepreneurship in Renewable Energy. *NBER*. Retrieved from http://www.nber.org/chapters/c13048

Navis, C., & Glynn, M. A. (2010). How New Market Categories Emerge: Temporal Dynamics of Legitimacy, Identity, and Entrepreneurship in Satellite Radio, 1990–2005. *Administrative Science Quarterly*, *55*(3), 439–471. https://doi.org/10.2189/asqu.2010.55.3.439

Negro, S. O., Alkemade, F., & Hekkert, M. P. (2012). Why does renewable energy diffuse so slowly? A review of innovation system problems. *Renewable and Sustainable Energy Reviews*, *16*(6), 3836–3846. https://doi.org/10.1016/j.rser.2012.03.043

Negro, S. O., & Hekkert, M. P. (2008). Explaining the success of emerging technologies by innovation system functioning: the case of biomass digestion in Germany. *Technology Analysis & Strategic Management*, *20*(4), 465–482. https://doi.org/10.1080/09537320802141437

Nelson, R. R. (1992). National Innovation Systems: A Retrospective on a Study. *Industrial and Corporate Change*, *2*, 347–374.

Nelson, R. R., & Winter, S. G. (1982). *An Evolutionary Theory of Economic Change*. Cambridge: Harvard University Press.

Neuendorf, K. A. (2002). *The content analysis guidebook*. Sage.

Niosi, J. (2011). Building innovation systems: an introduction to the special section. *Industrial and Corporate Change*, *20*(6), 1637–1643.

NREL. (2011). *2010 Solar Technologies Market Report*. National Renewable Energy Laboratory (NREL). Retrieved from http://www.nrel.gov/docs/fy12osti/51847.pdf

Oakey, R. (2003). Funding innovation and growth in UK new technology-based firms: Some observations on contributions from the public and private sectors. *Venture Capital*, *5*(2), 161–179. https://doi.org/10.1080/1369106032000097049

OECD. (2011). *Towards Green Growth*. Organisation for Economic Co-operation and Development (OECD).

OECD. (2013a). *OECD factbook: economic, environmental and social statistics.* OECD.

OECD. (2013b). *The Role of Banks, Equity Markets and Institutional Investors in Long-Term Financing for Growth and Development.* Paris.

Olmos, L., Ruester, S., & Liong, S.-J. (2012). On the selection of financing instruments to push the development of new technologies: Application to clean energy technologies. *Energy Policy*, *43*, 252–266. https://doi.org/10.1016/j.enpol.2012.01.001

O'Rourke, A. R. (2009). *The emergence of cleantech.* Yale University. Retrieved from http://gradworks.umi.com/33/61/3361640.html

O'Sullivan, M. (2005). Finance and innovation. In J. Fagerberg, D. C. Mowery, & R. R. Nelson (Eds.), *The Oxford Handbook of Innovation* (pp. 240–265). Oxford; New York: Oxford University Press, U.S.A.

Patton, M. Q. (2002). *Qualitative research and evaluation methods.* Thousand Oaks, CA: SAGE.

Peneder, M. (2010). The impact of venture capital on innovation behaviour and firm growth. *Venture Capital*, *12*(2), 83–107. https://doi.org/10.1080/13691061003643250

Penna, C. C. R., & Geels, F. W. (2012). Multi-dimensional struggles in the greening of industry: A dialectic issue lifecycle model and case study. *Technological Forecasting and Social Change*, *79*(6), 999–1020. https://doi.org/10.1016/j.techfore.2011.09.006

Perez, C. (2002a). *Technological revolutions and financial capital: The dynamics of bubbles and golden ages.* Cheltenham, UK: Edward Elgar Publishing.

Perez, C. (2002b). *Technological revolutions and financial capital: The dynamics of bubbles and golden ages.* Edward Elgar Publishing.

Pernick, R., & Wilder, C. (2007). *The Clean Tech Revolution: The Next Big Growth and Investment Opportunity.* New York, NY: Harper Business.

Peters, M., Schneider, M., Griesshaber, T., & Hoffmann, V. H. (2012a). The impact of technology-push and demand-pull policies on technical change – Does the locus of policies matter? *Research Policy*, *41*(8), 1296–1308. https://doi.org/10.1016/j.respol.2012.02.004

Peters, M., Schneider, M., Griesshaber, T., & Hoffmann, V. H. (2012b). The impact of technology-push and demand-pull policies on technical change – Does the locus of policies matter? *Research Policy*, *41*(8), 1296–1308. https://doi.org/10.1016/j.respol.2012.02.004

Petkova, A. P., Wadhwa, A., Yao, X., & Jain, S. (2014). Reputation and Decision Making under Ambiguity: A Study of U.S. Venture Capital Firms' Investments in the Emerging Clean Energy Sector. *Academy of Management Journal*, *57*(2), 422–448. https://doi.org/10.5465/amj.2011.0651

Phillips, N., Lawrence, T. B., & Hardy, C. (2004). Discourse and Institutions. *The Academy of Management Review*, *29*(4), 635–652. https://doi.org/10.2307/20159075

Pisano, G. P. (2010). The evolution of science-based business: innovating how we innovate. *Industrial and Corporate Change*, *19*(2), 465–482. https://doi.org/10.1093/icc/dtq013

Polzin, F., Migendt, M., Täube, F. A., & von Flotow, P. (2015). Public policy influence on renewable energy investments—A panel data study across OECD countries. *Energy Policy*, *80*, 98–111. https://doi.org/10.1016/j.enpol.2015.01.026

Polzin, F., von Flotow, P., & Klerkx, L. (2016). Addressing barriers to eco-innovation: Exploring the finance mobilisation functions of institutional innovation intermediaries. *Technological Forecasting and Social Change*, *103*, 34–46. https://doi.org/10.1016/j.techfore.2015.10.001

Popp, D., Hascic, I., & Medhi, N. (2011). Technology and the diffusion of renewable energy. *Energy Economics*, *33*(4), 648–662. https://doi.org/10.1016/j.eneco.2010.08.007

Porter, M. E. (1980). *Competitive strategies: Techniques for analyzing industries and competitors*. New York: Free Press.

PwC Moneytree. (2014). *Cleantech MoneyTree Report: Q4 2013*.

PwC Moneytree. (2015). *Cleantech MoneyTree Report: Q4 2014*.

Quirion, P. (2010). Complying with the Kyoto Protocol under uncertainty: Taxes or tradable permits? *Energy Policy*, *38*(9), 5166–5173.

Ragwitz, M., Held, A., Pfluger, B., Nuemann, K., Resch, G., Faber, T., & Wiser, R. (2008). *Assessment of the effectiveness of renewable energy support schemes in the BRICS countries*. Fraunhofer Institute Systems and Innovation Research, Karlsruhe/ Energy Economics Group, Vienna University of Technology, Vienna/ Lawrence Berkeley National Laboratory, Berkeley.

Randjelovic, J., O'Rourke, A. R., & Orsato, R. J. (2003). The Emergence of Green Venture Capital. *Business Strategy and the Environment*, *12*(4), 240–253. https://doi.org/10.1002/bse.361

Reed, W. R., & Ye, H. (2011). Which panel data estimator should I use? *Applied Economics*, *43*(8), 985–1000. https://doi.org/10.1080/00036840802600087

Revest, V., & Sapio, A. (2013). Does the alternative investment market nurture firm growth? A comparison between listed and private companies. *Industrial and Corporate Change*, *22*(4), 953–979. https://doi.org/10.1093/icc/dtt021

Rogge, K. S., & Hoffmann, V. H. (2010). The impact of the EU ETS on the sectoral innovation system for power generation technologies - Findings for Germany. *Energy Policy*, *38*(12), 7639–7652.

Rogge, K. S., Schneider, M., & Hoffmann, V. H. (2011). The innovation impact of the EU Emission Trading System — Findings of company case studies in the German power sector. *Ecological Economics*, *70*, 513–523.

Roth, G. (2012, August 9). Pension Giant CalPERS Appears Ready To Abandon Most VCs. Retrieved June 24, 2014, from http://www.pehub.com/2012/08/pension-giant-calpers-appears-ready-to-abandon-most-venture-capital-investing/

Samara, E., Georgiadis, P., & Bakouros, I. (2012). The impact of innovation policies on the performance of national innovation systems: A system dynamics analysis. *Technovation*, *32*(11), 624–638. https://doi.org/10.1016/j.technovation.2012.06.002

Samila, S., & Sorenson, O. (2010a). Venture capital as a catalyst to commercialization. *Research Policy*, *39*(10), 1348–1360. https://doi.org/10.1016/j.respol.2010.08.006

Samila, S., & Sorenson, O. (2010b). Venture Capital, Entrepreneurship, and Economic Growth. *Review of Economics and Statistics*, *93*(1), 338–349. https://doi.org/10.1162/REST_a_00066

Satyapal, S. (2014). *Annual Merit Review and Peer Evaluation Meeting*. U.S. Department of Energy Hydrogen & Fuel Cells Program. Retrieved from http://energy.gov/sites/prod/files/2014/07/f17/03_satyapal_plenary_2014_amr.pdf

Schiederig, T., Tietze, F., & Herstatt, C. (2012). Green innovation in technology and innovation management–an exploratory literature review. *R&D Management*, *42*(2), 180–192.

Schleich, J. (2009). Barriers to energy efficiency: A comparison across the German commercial and services sector. *Ecological Economics*, *68*(7), 2150–2159. https://doi.org/10.1016/j.ecolecon.2009.02.008

Schneider, C., & Veugelers, R. (2010). On young highly innovative companies: why they matter and how (not) to policy support them. *Industrial and Corporate Change*, *19*(4), 969–1007.

Schock, F. (2014). Private Equity Financing of Technology Firms: A Literature Review. *Alternative Investment Analyst Revew*, *3*(1), 19–48.

Schock, F., Mutl, J., Täube, F. A., & von Flotow, P. (2014). *Interdependencies between Technology and Capacity Investments in the Solar Technology Sector* (SSRN Scholarly Paper No. ID 2501857). Oestrich-Winkel: EBS Business School. Retrieved from http://papers.ssrn.com/abstract=2501857

Schumpeter, J. (1934). *The theory of economic development: An inquiry into profits, capital, credit, interest, and the business cycle* (Vol. 55). Transaction Publishers.

Schumpeter, J. (1942). *Capitalism, socialism and democracy*. London: Routledge.

Sine, W. D., & David, R. J. (2003). Environmental jolts, institutional change, and the creation of entrepreneurial opportunity in the US electric power industry. *Research Policy*, *32*(2), 185–207. https://doi.org/10.1016/S0048-7333(02)00096-3

Smith, A., Voß, J.-P., & Grin, J. (2010). Innovation studies and sustainability transitions: The allure of the multi-level perspective and its challenges. *Research Policy*, *39*(4), 435–448. https://doi.org/10.1016/j.respol.2010.01.023

Smith, S., & Swierzbinski, J. (2007). Assessing the performance of the UK Emissions Trading Scheme. *Environmental and Resource Economics*, *37*(1).

Sonntag-O'Brien, V., & Usher, E. (2004). Mobilizing finance for renewable energies. *Renewable Energy, A Global View of Technologies, Policies and Markets*, 169–195.

Soskice, D. (1997). German technology policy, innovation, and national institutional frameworks. *Industry & Innovation*, *4*(1), 75–96. https://doi.org/10.1080/13662719700000005

Steele, B. C. H., & Heinzel, A. (2001). Materials for fuel-cell technologies. *Nature*, *414*(6861), 345–352. https://doi.org/10.1038/35104620

Steinbach, A. (2013). Barriers and solutions for expansion of electricity grids—the German experience. *Energy Policy*, *63*, 224–229. https://doi.org/10.1016/j.enpol.2013.08.073

Stern, N. H. (2006). *Stern Review: The economics of climate change*. HM treasury London.

Stucki, T. (2014). Success of start-up firms: the role of financial constraints. *Industrial and Corporate Change*, *23*(1), 25–64. https://doi.org/10.1093/icc/dtt008

Szabó, S., & Jäger-Waldau, A. (2008). More competition: Threat or chance for financing renewable electricity? *Energy Policy*, *36*(4), 1436–1447.

Tampakis, S., Tsantopoulos, G., Arabatzis, G., & Rerras, I. (2013). Citizens' views on various forms of energy and their contribution to the environment. *Renewable and Sustainable Energy Reviews*, *20*, 473–482. https://doi.org/10.1016/j.rser.2012.12.027

Thomas, D. R. (2006). A General Inductive Approach for Analyzing Qualitative Evaluation Data. *American Journal of Evaluation*, *27*(2), 237–246. https://doi.org/10.1177/1098214005283748

Timmons, J. A., & Bygrave, W. D. (1986). Venture capital's role in financing innovation for economic growth. *Journal of Business Venturing*, *1*(2), 161–176. https://doi.org/10.1016/0883-9026(86)90012-1

Tsoutsos, T. D., & Stamboulis, Y. A. (2005). The sustainable diffusion of renewable energy technologies as an example of an innovation-focused policy. *Technovation*, *25*(7), 753–761. https://doi.org/10.1016/j.technovation.2003.12.003

UNEP. (2009). *Global Green New Deal – An Update for the G20 Pittsburgh Summit*. Pittsburgh. Retrieved from http://www.unep.org/pdf/G20_policy_brief_Final.pdf

Upreti, B. R. (2004). Conflict over biomass energy development in the United Kingdom: some observations and lessons from England and Wales. *Energy Policy*, *32*(6), 785–800. https://doi.org/10.1016/S0301-4215(02)00342-7

U.S. Department of Energy. (2014). *Comparison of Fuel Cell Technologies*. Retrieved from http://energy.gov/sites/prod/files/2014/08/f18/fcto_fuel_cells_comparison_chart.pdf

Uyarra, E. (2010). What is evolutionary about "regional systems of innovation"? Implications for regional policy. *Journal of Evolutionary Economics*, *20*(1), 115–137. https://doi.org/10.1007/s00191-009-0135-y

Van de Ven, A. H., & Garud, R. (1991). Innovation and industry development: The case of cochlear implants. *Research on Technological Innovation, Management and Policy*, *5*, 1–46.

Van de Ven, H. (1993). The development of an infrastructure for entrepreneurship. *Journal of Business Venturing*, *8*(3), 211–230. https://doi.org/10.1016/0883-9026(93)90028-4

Ventresca, M. J., & Mohr, J. W. (2002). Archival research methods. *The Blackwell Companion to Organizations*, 805–828.

Veugelers, R. (2011). *Europe's clean technology investment challenge* (Policy Contributions No. 561). Bruegel. Retrieved from http://ideas.repec.org/p/bre/polcon/561.html

Veugelers, R. (2012a). Which policy instruments to induce clean innovating? *Research Policy*, *41*(10), 1770–1778. https://doi.org/10.1016/j.respol.2012.06.012

Veugelers, R. (2012b). Which policy instruments to induce clean innovating? *Research Policy*, *41*(10), 1770–1778. https://doi.org/10.1016/j.respol.2012.06.012

von Burg, U., & Kenney, M. (2000). Venture capital and the birth of the local area networking industry. *Research Policy*, *29*(9), 1135–1155. https://doi.org/10.1016/S0048-7333(99)00072-4

Weber, K. M., & Rohracher, H. (2012). Legitimizing research, technology and innovation policies for transformative change: Combining insights from innovation systems and multi-level perspective in a comprehensive "failures" framework. *Research Policy*, *41*(6), 1037–1047. https://doi.org/10.1016/j.respol.2011.10.015

Weber, R. P. (1990). *Basic content analysis*. Newbury Park, CA: Sage.

White, S., Gao, J., & Zhang, W. (2005). Financing new ventures in China: System antecedents and institutionalization. *Research Policy*, *34*(6), 894–913. https://doi.org/10.1016/j.respol.2005.04.002

White, W., Lunnan, A., Nybakk, E., & Kulisic, B. (2013). The role of governments in renewable energy: The importance of policy consistency. *Biomass and Bioenergy*, *57*, 97–105. https://doi.org/10.1016/j.biombioe.2012.12.035

Wonglimpiyarat, J. (2011). The dynamics of financial innovation system. *The Journal of High Technology Management Research*, *22*(1), 36–46.

Wooldridge, J. M., Calhoun, J. W., Jung, B., Greber, S., & Montgomery, R. (2009). *Introductory Econometrics* (4th ed.). Mason, OH: South-Western Cengage Learning.

Woolley, J. (2011). Studying the Emergence of New Organizations: Entrepreneurship Research Design. *Entrepreneurship Research Journal*, *1*(1).

Wright, M., Gilligan, J., & Amess, K. (2009). The economic impact of private equity: what we know and what we would like to know. *Venture Capital*, *11*(1), 1–21.

Wright, M., Pruthi, S., & Lockett, A. (2005). International venture capital research: From cross-country comparisons to crossing borders. *International Journal of Management Reviews*, *7*(3), 135–165.

Wright, M., & Robbie, K. (1998). Venture Capital and Private Equity: A Review and Synthesis. *Journal of Business Finance & Accounting*, *25*(5/6), 521–570.

Wüstenhagen, R., & Bilharz, M. (2006a). Green energy market development in Germany: effective public policy and emerging customer demand. *Energy Policy*, *34*(13), 1681–1696. https://doi.org/10.1016/j.enpol.2004.07.013

Wüstenhagen, R., & Bilharz, M. (2006b). Green energy market development in Germany: effective public policy and emerging customer demand. *Energy Policy*, *34*, 1681–1696.

Wüstenhagen, R., & Menichetti, E. (2012). Strategic choices for renewable energy investment: Conceptual framework and opportunities for further research. *Energy Policy*, *40*, 1–10. https://doi.org/10.1016/j.enpol.2011.06.050

Wüstenhagen, R., & Teppo, T. (2006). Do Venture Capitalists really Invest in Good Industries? Risk-Return Perceptions and Path Dependence in the Emerging European Energy VC Market. *International Journal of Technology Management*, *34*(1), 63–87.

Wüstenhagen, R., Wolsink, M., & Bürer, M. J. (2007). Social acceptance of renewable energy innovation: An introduction to the concept. *Energy Policy*, *35*, 2683–2691.

Wuthnow, R. (1989). *Communities of Discourse*. Cambridge, MA: Harvard University Press.

Yin, R. K. (2009). *Case study research: Design and methods* (Vol. 5). Thousand Oaks, CA: Sage Publications, Inc.

8 Appendix

8.1 Appendix to chapter 2

Cleantech
- Cleantech* (1)
- Greentech* (1)
- Clean-Tech* (1)
- Green-Tech* (1)

Other Cleantech
- Renewable Energ* (1)
- Sustain* Energ* (1)
- Hydro Energ* (1)
- Hydropower (1)
- Marine Energ* (1)
- Geothermal (1)
- On-site Systems (1)
- Hydrogen (1)
- Combined Heat (1)
- Combined Power (1)

Ecology
- Ecolog* (1)
- Eco-log* (1)

Sustainable Transportation
- Electric Vehicle* (1)
- Hybrid Vehicle* (1)
- Electric Car* (1)
- Hybrid Car* (1)
- Electric Engine* (1)
- Electric Auto* (1)

Biofuels & Biomaterials
- Biofuel* (1)
- Biomaterial* (1)
- Biodiesel (1)
- Biomass (1)
- Grain Ethanol (1)
- Cellulosic Ethanol (1)
- Biogas (1)
- Algae Biogas (1)

Sustainable Agriculture
- Sustainable Agriculture (1)
- Land Management (1)
- Natural Pesticide* (1)
- Crop Yield (1)
- Sustainable Fertilizer* (1)
- Precision Agriculture (1)

Solar
- Solar (1)
- Solar System* (1)
- Solar Cell* (1)
- Solar Module* (1)
- Thin Film* (1)
- Photovoltaic* (1)
- Concentrated PV (1)
- Concentrated Solar Thermal (1)
- Electric Cell* (1)
- Photovoltaic Cell* (1)

Water Energy
- Water Treatment (1)
- Wastewater Treatment (1)
- Purification (1)
- Filtration (1)
- Water Conservation (1)

Air & Environment
- Emission* (1)
- Emissions Control (1)
- Carbon* (1)
- Clean Coal (1)

Wind Energy
- Wind Farm* (1)
- Wind Turbine* (1)
- Wind Energy Facilit* (1)
- Wind Park* (1)
- Wind Turbine (1)

Materials
- clean Bio* (1)
- clean Nano* (1)
- clean Chemical* (1)
- clean Polymer* (1)
- Biodegradable (1)
- Sustain* Product* (1)

Recycling & Waste
- Recycling (1)
- Waste to Energ* (1)
- Mixed Waste* (1)
- Waste Treatment* (1)

Energy Efficiency
- Energy Efficiency (1)
- Energy Monitoring (1)
- Building Envelope (1)
- Building Insulation (1)
- Building Automation (1)
- HVAC (1)

Energy Storage
- Energy Storage (1)
- Advanced Batter* (1)
- Fuel Cell* (1)
- Energy Storage (1)
- Lithium-Ion (1)
- Battery Charging (1)

Smart Grid
- Smart Grid (1)
- Energy Infrastructure (1)
- Transmission Management (1)

Figure 21 – Cleantech dictionary

8.2 Appendix to chapter 3

Innovation policy	Innovators (I)	VC/PE	Institutional Investors (II)
Geographical area	*Relation 1a*	*Relation 1b*	*Relations 1c*
Common	"The government shouldn't be in the business of picking winners and losers. They're not smart enough, they aren't good VCs, they aren't even equity firms so that constitutes a problem" (USA22 - Innovator) ——— "If there is a very capital-intensive business in a low-growth industry, and it relies on subsidies [...], if they go away, the company disappears. For Cleantech, it is a deal-breaker if the business model is reliant on subsidies" (GER10 – Private Equity Investor) ——— "Some steady state of affairs in policy making is a better scenario it seems to	"[Clean technology VCs] are struggling to raise capital because the returns aren't good" (USA20 – Institutional Investor) ——— In my opinion regulatory frameworks are overrated in their importance for innovative companies. (GER1 – Private Equity Investor)	"The institutional investors engaged in the field are hesitant to pursue further investments until previous investments are returned and positive results are realized" (USA20 – Institutional Investor)

	me" (USA19 – Policy maker) "The government is trying to make sure we grow the innovation base and provides a source of capital to get products out of the classroom to the market" (USA6 – Policy maker)		
USA	"There are plenty of companies that do really good business without regulatory support or feed-in tariffs" (GER11 – Institutional Investor) "So I think that it is not that the government is picking winners and losers per se; in fact, it is the government essentially offering low-cost financing to projects the private sector has already picked in an effort to get a new industry off the ground" (USA19 – Policy maker)	"The reason behind [the involvement of private investors] is that you want the private capital markets to tell you which projects they are supporting" (USA19 – Policy maker)	"Back in 2004, the Green Wave initiative that was started over at the state capitol came across to CalPERS and CalSTRS and […] it was decided to put $200 million into the Cleantech space across a number of managers" (USA20 – Institutional Investor) "So our total exposure […] is $1.5 billion approximately. It's a very big program, and we have actually now stopped investing in clean technology directly because we're waiting to see how things work" (USA20 – Institutional Investor)

	"The most unsuccessful program without question has been the loan guarantee program. There's no doubt about it" (USA17 – Private Equity Investor)		
	"The political environment isn't very supportive of our technology. So we have never developed a business plan that relies on government support" (USA3 – Innovator)		
	"in the US there is really no regulatory inputs [on greenhouse gas emissions] at all for most of our companies" (USA18 – Private Equity Investor)		
GER	"When Germany came up with the feed-in tariff program is when solar really took off" (USA11 – Private Equity Investor)	"Governments increasingly see venture capital as a tool of industrial policy and therefore […] around most governments in Europe, venture capital is a good thing, same at EU	"Real asset investing does not really have any upsides, but investors like it because its risks resemble fixed income investing" (GER11 – Institutional Investor)

	"The subsidy environment and the understanding of the need for renewable energy is so much lower in the United States versus Germany" (USA12 – Policy maker)	level" (GER15 – Venture Capital Investor) "You can create all the policy framework you like in terms of trying to create a venture capital industry, but unless you're releasing local sources of capital for that, it will never succeed" (GER13 – Institutional Investor)	

Table 14 – Innovation policy (direct and indirect) effects

Financial policy	**Institutional Investors (II)**	**VC/PE**	**Innovators (I)**
Geographical area	*Relation 2a*	*Relation 2b*	*Relation 2c*
Common	"The threat of that [regulations to cover capital adequacy], I think, is quite profound so if a pension fund or an insurance company needs to reserve capital differently because it invests in a higher risk asset classes, you are clearly going to do less of it" (GER15 – Venture Capital Investor)	"[Fund-of-funds] add an extra fee layer [… / and] because they spread the money widely your returns will be fairly average" (GER15 – Venture Capital Investor)	"The Cleantech business does not easily match the business ecosystem of venture capital. It is capital intensive, it's highly illiquid and […] the money is locked up for long periods of time" (*USA 19 – Policy maker – IP*)

			"If a capital source has internal rate of return as a metric for their investment performance then they are going to have a hard time in Cleantech until the later stages where commercial feasibility has been proved" (USA – Institutional Investor)
			"you can create all the policy framework you like in terms of trying to create a venture capital industry, but unless you're releasing local sources of capital for that, it will never succeed." (GER13 – Institutional Investor)
USA	A lot of the banks who we thought would give us capital, didn't give us capital because they're dealing with their own capital issues, so that's clearly something that affected us in our fundraising. We don't have a single bank	One rule: No strings attached. If there is a connected regulation to public money to only invest locally or into very specific companies, leading funds will never take it. So only the worse investors take this kind of money and achieve worse returns.	

	invested in our fund, versus a few years ago, some of our competitors had investments from banks. So that's an example of where the institutional investor maybe can't do certain things now, that they could do a few years ago (USA17 – Private Equity Investor)	(GER10 – Private Equity Investor)	
GER	"The ability to release and liberate the pensions to invest in the asset class [VC/PE] is one of the most important policy changes that could be made within our region [Europe]" (GER13 – Institutional Investor) Public investors like the EIF or the KfW almost have a monopoly. They decide where the money goes in VC. This publicly supported monopoly needs to get abolished (USA 21 - Institutional Investor)	"A successful industry, particularly in [the view of] venture capital is about scale and size, and so in a sense there's a dangerous spiral that you can get into actually where you have to recreate certain parts of an entire industry that's been built up over 15 years from scratch" (GER13 – Institutional Investor) "[Institutional] investors don't really want to get out of bed for a small ticket" (GER13 – Institutional Investor) "The cut of the tax loss	"In our typical exit, we sell the company to a larger buyout fund at the end of our holding period" (GER1 – Private Equity Investor)

		carry-forward after a bigger investment round or after a sale makes all the investments of a company or indirectly a fund lost. I can't get all the losses from the past back. Therefore an investor who supported some research is systematically disadvantaged against corporates" (GER16 – Venture Capital Investor)	

Table 15 – Financial policy (direct and indirect) effects

Code	Role	Type	Date	# Interviewers	Contact
GER1	Managing Partner	PE GER	Q4 - 2011	2	Face-to-face
GER2	CFO	Company GER	Q4 - 2011	1	Face-to-face
GER3	CEO & Founder	Company GER	Q4 - 2011	2	Face-to-face
GER4	Chairman	PE GER	Q4 - 2011	2	Face-to-face
GER5	Director	Public GER	Q4 - 2011	2	
GER6	Principal	LP GER	Q4 - 2011	2	Phone
GER7	Department Head	Public GER	Q4 - 2011	1	Phone
USA1	Head of Communications	Public USA	Q4 - 2011	2	Face-to-face
USA2	Chief Marketing Officer, Founder	Company USA	Q4 - 2011	2	Face-to-face
USA3	President & CEO	Company USA	Q4 - 2011	2	Face-to-face
USA4	Managing Partner	PE USA	Q4 - 2011	2	Face-to-face
USA5	President & CEO	Company USA	Q4 - 2011	2	Face-to-face
USA6	Program Manager	Public USA	Q4 - 2011	2	Face-to-face
USA7	CEO	Company USA	Q4 - 2011	2	Face-to-face
USA8	Department Head	Public USA	Q4 - 2011	2	Face-to-face
USA9	CEO	LP USA	Q4 - 2011	2	Face-to-face
USA10	Managing Partner	VC USA	Q4 - 2011	2	Face-to-face
USA11	Managing Partner	PE USA	Q4 - 2011	2	Face-to-face
USA12	Manager Consulting Services	Public USA	Q4 - 2011	2	Face-to-face
USA13	CEO	Company USA	Q4 - 2011	2	Face-to-face
USA14	CEO	Company USA	Q4 - 2011	2	Face-to-face
USA15	President & CEO	Company USA	Q4 - 2011	2	Face-to-face
USA16	Managing Partner	PE USA	Q4 - 2011	2	Face-to-face
GER8	Partner	PE GER	Q1 - 2012	1	Phone
GER9	Investment Manager	PE GER	Q1 - 2012	2	Face-to-face
GER10	Investment Associate	PE GER	Q1 - 2012	2	Face-to-face
GER11	Head of Private Equity	LP GER	Q1 - 2012	2	Face-to-face
GER12	CFO	Company GER	Q1 - 2012	2	Face-to-face
GER13	Senior Investor	LP GER	Q1 - 2012	2	Face-to-face
GER14	Investment Associate	PE GER	Q1 - 2012	2	Face-to-face
GER15	Partner	VC GER	Q1 - 2012	2	Face-to-face
USA17	Head of Energy Investments	PE USA	Q1 - 2012	2	Phone

GER16	Partner	VC GER	Q1 - 2012	3	Face-to-face
GER17	Partner	VC GER	Q1 - 2012	3	Face-to-face
USA18	ESG Professional	PE USA	Q2 - 2012	1	Phone
USA19	Department Head	Public USA	Q2 - 2012	2	Phone
USA20	Portfolio Manager	LP USA	Q2 - 2012	2	Face-to-face
USA21	President	LP USA	Q2 - 2012	2	Face-to-face
USA22	CEO	Company USA	Q2 - 2012	2	Phone
USA23	Head of Practice	LP USA	Q2 - 2012	2	Face-to-face
USA24	CEO	Company USA	Q2 - 2012	2	Face-to-face
USA25	Investment Partner	VC USA	Q2 - 2012	2	Face-to-face
USA26	Senior Project Manager	Public USA	Q2 - 2012	1	Face-to-face
USA27	CEO	Company USA	Q2 - 2012	2	Phone
USA28	General Partner	VC USA	Q2 - 2012	2	Face-to-face
GER18	Senior Vice President Finance	Company GER	Q2 - 2012	2	Face-to-face
USA29	Vice Presisident Sales	VC USA	Q2 - 2012	2	Face-to-face
GER19	Founder & Chairman	VC GER	Q2 - 2012	2	Face-to-face
USA30	Partner	VC USA	Q3 - 2012	2	Phone
GER20	Head of Venture Capital	LP GER	Q3 - 2012	2	Face-to-face
USA31	Senior Policy Advisor	Public USA	Q3 - 2012	2	Face-to-face
USA32	Principal	VC USA	Q3 - 2012	2	Face-to-face
USA33	Investment Manager	VC USA	Q3 - 2012	2	Face-to-face
USA34	Partner	VC USA	Q3 - 2012	2	Face-to-face
USA35	Director	Public USA	Q3 - 2012	2	Face-to-face
USA36	Co-Head	Public USA	Q3 - 2012	2	Face-to-face
GER21	Comissioner	Public GER	Q3 - 2012	2	Face-to-face
USA37	Investment Manager	VC USA	Q3 - 2012	2	Face-to-face
USA38	Princial	VC USA	Q3 - 2012	2	Face-to-face
USA39	CEO	Company USA	Q3 - 2012	2	Face-to-face
USA40	Founder & Chairman	Company USA	Q3 - 2012	2	Face-to-face
USA41	Investment Manager	VC USA	Q3 - 2012	2	Face-to-face
GER22	Partner	Public GER	Q4 - 2012	2	Phone
GER23	CEO	Company GER	Q4 - 2012	2	Phone

Table 16 – Detailed interview descriptives

Appendix: Sample questionnaire

Questionnaire Type: Investor

Questions:

1. **Personal background**

- What is your educational/professional background?
- What is your current position in your investment firm? (e.g. Partner, Investment Manager)
- What are your responsibilities in your investment firm?
- How long have you been working for your investment firm?
- How long have you been working in the investment industry?

2. **Investment firm background**

- Describe the history, structure and size of your investment partnership/funds.
- Who are your limited partners and according to your knowledge what were the main reasons for their commitment to your fund?
- Did your limited partners influence the selection of the sectors you have invested in?
- In which sectors or subsectors does your firm invest?
- What are the reasons for investing or not investing in the cleantech sector?

3. **Investment process**

- What is the typical size of your total investment in a company and the typical investment round?
- At the time you first invest in a portfolio company, what is your intended investment horizon or holding period?
- In which stage or stages of the corporate life cycle do you invest? (e.g. start-up, early stage, expansion stage, later stage)
- How many business plans or companies do you review per month, how many of them are considered in more detail an how many are selected for an investment?
- What is the average time you spend on portfolio companies per month and with what tasks are you occupied in this time?
- What are important criteria that you look for in a company that you would like to invest in?
- What are common deal breakers that you encounter during the investment process?

- Are there any hard (economic or financial) factors that rule out certain investments?
- What is your attitude towards technology risk?

4. Investment environment

- How do you evaluate the current political and regulatory environment for *institutional investors* and to which degree is it influencing your investment activity?
- How do you evaluate the current political and regulatory environment for the *alternative investment/private equity sector* and to which degree is it influencing your investment activity?
- How do you evaluate the current political and regulatory investment environment in the *renewable energy and "clean" technology sector* and to which degree is it influencing your investment activity?
- How do you evaluate the investment opportunities in companies vis-à-vis asset/project finance?
- Which government programs or actions do you consider particularly successful or not successful?
- What are your suggestions for a more prosperous investment environment?

5. Investment challenges

- What are the three most dominant challenges your investment firm is facing in the current environment?

8.3 Appendix to chapter 4

Countries included in Multiple RE	Countries included in Solar	Countries included in Wind	Countries included in Biomass
Australia, Austria, Belgium, Canada, Chile, Czech Republic, Denmark, Estonia, Finland, France, Germany, Greece, Hungary, Ireland, Italy, Japan, Korea, Rep., Mexico, Netherlands, New Zealand, Norway, Poland, Portugal, Slovak Republic, Spain, Sweden, Switzerland, Turkey, United Kingdom, United States	Australia, Belgium, Canada, Czech Republic, France, Germany, Greece, Italy, Japan, Korea, Rep., Netherlands, Portugal, Slovak Republic, Spain, Turkey, United Kingdom, United States	Australia, Austria, Belgium, Canada, Chile, Czech Republic, Denmark, Estonia, Finland, France, Germany, Greece, Hungary, Ireland, Italy, Japan, Korea, Rep., Mexico, Netherlands, New Zealand, Norway, Poland, Portugal, Spain, Sweden, Switzerland, Turkey, United Kingdom, United States	Australia, Austria, Belgium, Canada, Chile, Czech Republic, Finland, France, Germany, Ireland, Italy, Japan, Mexico, Netherlands, Norway, Poland, Spain, Sweden, United Kingdom, United States

Table 17 – Country selection

Category	Variable	Definition	Source	Obs.	Mean	Std. Dev.	Min	Max
	$BNEF\_Capacity\_ALL_{jk}$	Logarithm of the installed capacity additions of multiple renewable energy sources (aggregated from $BNEF\_Capacity\_Biomass_{jk}$, $BNEF\_Capacity\_Solar_{jk}$, $BNEF\_Capacity\_Wind_{jk}$)	Bloomberg New Energy Finance (BNEF)	360	3.61	2.81	0	9.43
Dependent variables	$BNEF\_Capacity\_Biomass_{jk}$	Logarithm of the installed capacity additions of biomass capacity	idem	240	2.25	2.09	0	6.80
	$BNEF\_Capacity\_Solar_{jk}$	Logarithm of the installed capacity additions of solar capacity	idem	192	1.76	2.27	0	8.56
	$BNEF\_Capacity\_Wind_{jk}$	Logarithm of the installed capacity additions of wind capacity	idem	348	3.34	2.81	0	9.17
	$EI\_FI\_FI_{jk}$	Logarithm of ANPM (Feed-in tariffs/premiums)	IEA policies and measures database	360	0.48	0.52	0	1.95
Economic Instruments – Fiscal/financial incentives (EI_FI)	$EI\_FI\_GS_{jk}$	Logarithm of ANPM (Grants and subsidies)	idem	360	0.88	0.64	0	2.30
	$EI\_FI\_L_{jk}$	Logarithm of ANPM (Loans)	idem	360	0.25	0.38	0	1.61
	$EI\_FI\_TR_{jk}$	Logarithm of ANPM (Tax relief)	idem	360	0.40	0.52	0	1.79
	$EI\_FI\_T_{jk}$	Logarithm of ANPM (Taxes)	idem	360	0.27	0.37	0	1.10
Economic Instruments – Market-based instruments (EI_MI)	$EI\_MI\_GA_{jk}$	Logarithm of ANPM (GHG emissions allowances)	idem	360	0.10	0.29	0	1.39
	$EI\_MI\_GC_{jk}$	Logarithm of ANPM (Green certificates)	idem	360	0.19	0.37	0	1.61
Economic Instruments - Direct investment (EI_DI)	$EI\_DI\_FSG_{jk}$	Logarithm of ANPM (Funds to sub-national governments)	idem	360	0.16	0.32	0	1.39
	$EI\_DI\_II_{jk}$	Logarithm of ANPM (Infrastructure investments)	idem	360	0.17	0.36	0	1.60

Policy Support (PS)	PS_IC_{jk}	Logarithm of ANPM (Institutional creation)	idem	360	0.47	0.49	0	1.95
	PS_SP_{jk}	Logarithm of ANPM (Strategic planning)	idem	360	0.87	0.56	0	2.08
Regulatory Instruments (RI)	RI_CS_{jk}	Logarithm of ANPM (Codes and standards)	idem	360	0.51	0.52	0	2.40
	RI_OS_{jk}	Logarithm of ANPM (Obligation schemes)	idem	360	0.64	0.51	0	2.08
	RI_MR_{jk}	Logarithm of ANPM (Other mandatory requirements)	idem	360	0.46	0.56	0	2.30
Control variables	c_TEC_{jk}	Logarithm of total energy consumption	World bank	360	3.50	1.18	1.23	6.96
	c_CI_{jk}	Logarithm of CO2 intensity – Metric tons of carbon dioxide per thousand year 2005 U.S. dollars GDP	EIA	360	0.34	0.17	0.10	0.99
	c_LIR_{jk}	Logarithm of long-term interest rates	OECD	360	1.52	0.60	0	2.82
	c_SP_{jk}	Logarithm of share prices (index)	OECD	360	4.49	0.49	2.90	5.70
	c_GDP_{jk}	Logarithm of real gross domestic product (in billions U.S. dollars, 2013)	World bank	360	26.72	2.00	0	30.34

Table 18 – Data: definition, sources and descriptive statistics

Variables	IC	EI_FI_FI	EI_FI_GS	EI_FI_L	EI_FI_TR	EI_FI_T	EI_MI_GA	EI_MI_GC	EI_DI_~G	EI_DI_II	PS_IC	PS_SP	RI_CS	RI_OS	RI_MR	c_TEC	c_CI	c_LIR	c_SP	c_GDP
IC	1.00																			
EI_FI_FI	0.15	1.00																		
EI_FI_GS	0.26	0.21	1.00																	
EI_FI_L	0.23	0.11	0.17	1.00																
EI_FI_TR	0.33	0.09	0.22	0.34	1.00															
EI_FI_T	0.09	-0.01	0.07	0.28	0.07	1.00														
EI_MI_GA	0.20	-0.26	0.01	0.22	0.08	0.57	1.00													
EI_MI_GC	0.18	-0.17	-0.05	0.19	0.19	0.23	0.27	1.00												
EI_DI_FSG	0.14	-0.14	0.28	0.25	0.23	0.19	0.04	-0.09	1.00											
EI_DI_II	0.11	0.10	0.36	0.23	0.26	0.02	-0.05	0.02	0.06	1.00										
PS_IC	0.18	0.22	0.34	0.32	-0.01	0.19	0.14	-0.14	0.08	0.27	1.00									
PS_SP	0.29	-0.03	0.26	0.34	-0.01	0.34	0.41	0.37	0.26	0.05	0.40	1.00								
RI_CS	0.32	0.10	0.38	0.25	0.44	0.23	0.05	0.22	0.34	0.29	0.27	0.30	1.00							
RI_OS	0.36	0.08	0.23	0.17	0.30	0.01	0.20	-0.00	0.17	0.08	0.46	0.15	0.34	1.00						
RI_MR	0.33	-0.11	0.07	0.41	0.45	0.18	0.08	0.16	0.40	0.26	0.03	0.15	0.40	0.40	1.00					
c_TEC	0.40	-0.12	0.30	0.31	0.38	0.04	0.19	0.06	0.39	0.13	0.19	0.13	0.30	0.45	0.53	1.00				
c_CI	-0.17	-0.04	-0.18	-0.17	-0.10	-0.22	-0.19	-0.13	-0.18	0.08	-0.19	-0.34	-0.16	-0.00	0.01	-0.26	1.00			
c_LIR	-0.01	0.08	0.16	0.16	0.15	0.25	0.10	0.13	0.09	0.17	0.16	0.18	0.22	0.12	0.11	0.05	-0.28	1.00		
c_SP	0.31	0.27	0.19	0.21	0.20	0.19	0.05	0.22	0.08	0.01	0.26	0.37	0.24	0.22	0.10	0.07	-0.33	0.24	1.00	
c_GDP	0.37	0.02	0.23	0.21	0.32	0.09	0.16	0.16	0.17	0.10	0.10	0.10	0.31	0.33	0.39	0.70	-0.31	0.07	0.16	1.00

Table 19 – Pairwise correlation coefficients (Multiple RE /aggregated sectors)

Independent variables (ANPM) (t-1)	Random effects							
	CSE		CSE		CSE		CSE	
	Multiple RE		Wind		Solar		Biomass	
	(IX)		(X)		(XI)		(XII)	
	Coeff.	S.E.	Coeff.	S.E.	Coeff.	S.E.	Coeff.	S.E.
$EI\_FI\_FI_{jk}$	0.65*	0.38	0.61*	0.36	1.18***	0.31	0.09	0.26
$EI\_FI\_GS_{jk}$	0.98***	0.36	0.83**	0.36	0.61**	0.25	0.61***	0.25
$EI\_FI\_L_{jk}$	-0.38	0.55	0.66	0.53	-0.91**	0.43	-0.15	0.39
$EI\_FI\_TR_{jk}$	0.36	0.43	-0.02	0.42	-0.01	0.34	0.10	0.27
$EI\_FI\_T_{jk}$	-1.43**	0.59	-0.50	0.58	1.00*	0.58	-0.20	0.39
$EI\_MI\_GA_{jk}$	2.06***	0.80	1.46*	0.83	-1.17	0.80	0.97**	0.53
$EI\_MI\_GC_{jk}$	0.15	0.56	0.24	0.52	-2.27***	0.48	0.06	0.37
$EI\_DI\_FSG_{jk}$	-1.12	0.71	-1.11	0.70	-1.43***	0.47	1.51***	0.52
$EI\_DI\_II_{jk}$	0.12	0.52	0.52	0.46	0.21	0.56	-1.20***	0.46
PS_IC_{jk}	-0.55	0.48	0.02	0.45	-1.51***	0.43	0.83**	0.36
PS_SP_{jk}	1.20***	0.42	0.66	0.43	2.35***	0.34	-0.44	0.30
RI_CS_{jk}	0.82*	0.48	1.03**	0.47	0.54	0.36	-0.41	0.33
RI_OS_{jk}	0.35	0.48	0.26	0.47	0.16	0.41	-0.01	0.34
RI_MR_{jk}	0.73	0.46	0.04	0.43	0.77	0.47	0.28	0.31
Control variables								
c_TEC_{jk}	0.62**	0.28	0.83	0.30	0.95	0.72	-1.97***	0.52
c_CI_{jk}	-0.66	1.60	-0.38	1.80	-6.01**	2.58	4.37***	1.60
c_LIR_{jk}	-0.71**	0.31	-0.75**	0.31	-0.54	0.67	-0.57*	0.30
c_SP_{jk}	1.84***	0.36	1.92***	0.37	-0.24	0.46	0.61*	0.37
c_GDP_{jk}	-0.04	0.08	-0.05	0.08	-0.82	0.70	2.16***	0.50
_cons	-7.54***	2.79	-8.64***	2.80	21.59	17.02	-53.24***	11.51
Observations	330		319		176		220	
R2	0.36		0.36		0.49		0.38	
Wald	205.74***		198.02***		152.19***		123.86***	

Notes: The Wald test has a Chi^2 distribution and tests the null hypothesis of non-significance of all coefficients of independent variables. Conventional standard errors (CSE) are reported. ***, **, *, denote significance at 1, 5 and 10% significance levels, Estimations include both country and time dummies. (Marques and Fuinhas, 2012a) xtreg command was used.

Table 20 – Random effects estimator (REE) regression results

8.4 Appendix to chapter 5

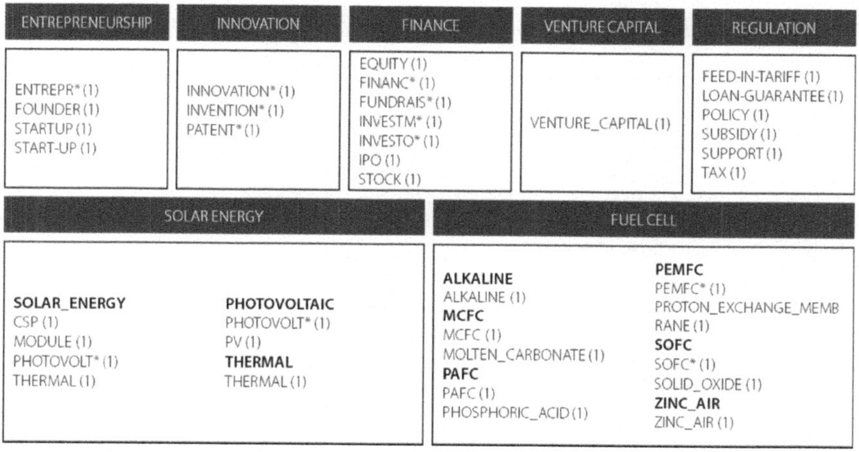

Figure 22 – Dictionaries used on articles

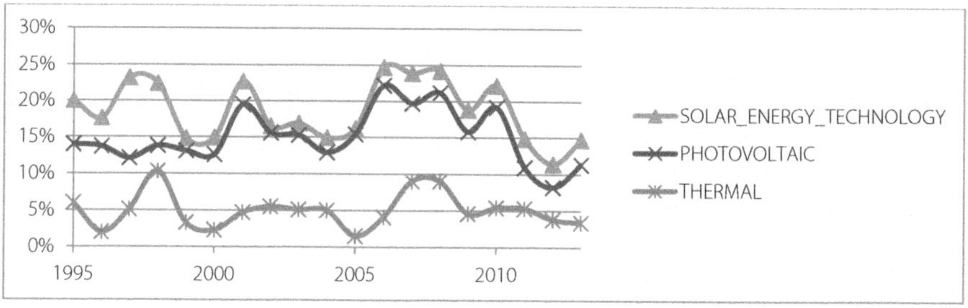

Figure 23 – Technology frames "solar energy"

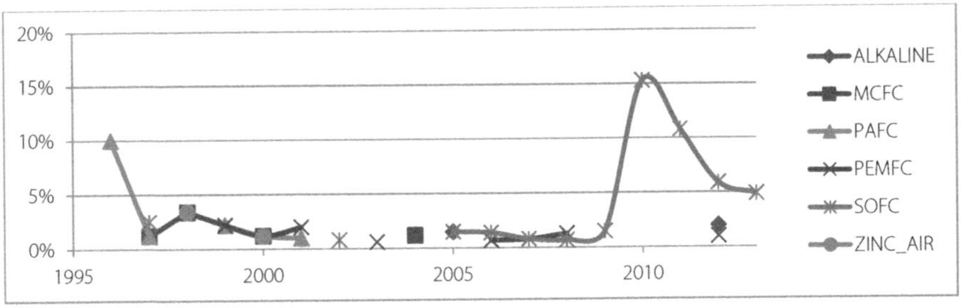

Figure 24 – Technology frames "fuel cell"

The manufacturer's authorised representative in the EU is Springer Nature Customer Service Centre GmbH, Europaplatz 3, 69115 Heidelberg, Germany. If you have any concerns regarding our products, please contact ProductSafety@springernature.com

Printed and bound by CPI Group (UK) Ltd, Croydon, CR0 4YY
25/09/2026
02222849-0012